W0009331

CRETE

THE WHITE MOUNTAINS

By

Loraine Wilson

CICERONE PRESS
MILNTHORPE, CUMBRIA
www.cicerone.co.uk

© Loraine Wilson 2000 Reprinted 2002
ISBN 1 85284 298 9
A catalogue record for this book is available from the British Library
All Photographs, Route Profiles and legend by the Author

ACKNOWLEDGEMENTS

My special thanks for their hospitality and friendship over many years of outdoor adventuring goes out to Olga Heliodakis of the Hotel Dictina, Angeliko Yalidakis of Askyfou, Theodoros Athitaki of Anopolis and Loula Dracoulakis of The New Omalos Hotel; to Andreas Stavroudaki of Ay. Roumeli for answering our endless questions about the fascinating Samaria Gorge; to Chania taxi driver Mr. Roussos who, with unfailing good humour, transports us to unusual places; to Pavlos, the Anopolis bus driver who toots his horn as a welcome each year. These, and many other Cretans, have welcomed me and my groups as special people, so that western Crete, although entirely different, always seems like a home from home.

Similarly, my gratitude for their interest goes to sociologist Sean Damer who studied the shepherding community of Askyfou; to my companions on many treks, Geoffrey Shaw and Roger de Freitas, for enriching the standard trekking product, not only with enthusiasm for exploring new routes, but with a more in-depth approach; for their gifts of books, for mentioning book-writing years ago, and for proof-reading the route notes. To my colleague in trekking, Ann Sainsbury, for proof-reading, and to Gail Wilson for supplying the workstation for writing.

**This book is dedicated to all those who love
the Lefka Ori and the south coast of Sfakia.**

Advice to readers

Readers are advised that whilst every effort is taken by the author to ensure the accuracy of this guidebook, changes can occur which may affect the contents. It is advisable to check locally on transport, accommodation, shops etc. but even rights of way can be altered and, more especially overseas, paths can be eradicated by landslip, forest fires or changes of ownership.

The publishers would welcome notice of any such changes.

Front cover: *A September view of the Niato plateau, showing the ascent route up Kastro (Walks 27 and 28)*

CONTENTS

2 ROUTE NOTES

3 MOUNTAIN WALKS
The Omalos Plateau

Northern Foothills (see also Walks 10a, 10b and 11a)

The Askyfou Plateau

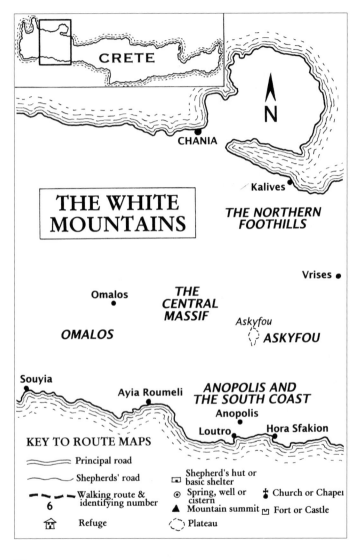

THE WHITE MOUNTAINS

CRETE

N

CHANIA

Kalives

THE NORTHERN FOOTHILLS

Vrises

Omalos

THE CENTRAL MASSIF

OMALOS

Askyfou

ASKYFOU

Souyia

Ayia Roumeli

ANOPOLIS AND THE SOUTH COAST

Anopolis

Loutro

Hora Sfakion

KEY TO ROUTE MAPS

〜〜〜 Principal road

〜 Shepherds' road

▬ ▬ ▬ Walking route & identifying number
6

⌂ Refuge

▱ Shepherd's hut or basic shelter

⊙ Spring, well or cistern

▲ Mountain summit

⌬ Plateau

✝ Church or Chapel

⌑ Fort or Castle

PREFACE

Six mountain ranges make up the backbone of the island, but quite the best is the Lefka Ori, or White Mountains, where several peaks rise to over 2,100m (7,000ft). Five good walking centres that are connected one with the other by bus or boat are also easily reached by bus from Chania. All are within 2 hours journey of the airport. There is plenty of good accommodation in the mountains, which does not have to be pre-booked. Most of the best walks are not circuits so that a hired car gets in the way, especially as much of the south coast, having no roads, is served by boat.

The White Mountains' many spectacular limestone features are so packed in that route-finding is quite daunting. Thirteen huge gorges split the southern flank, which rises steeply above the south coast. Elsewhere more ravines, forested crags and high-level plains add to the mass – and everywhere there are rocks, so that the underfoot is as rugged as any you will find.

High above the gorges and the tree line, snow thaws by July to reveal an entirely different landscape. A dozen massive, shadeless, scree-surfaced peaks, interspersed with forbidding 'moonscape' valleys, form a unique and unforgettable desert wilderness. Shimmering in a waterless heat haze, old trails are enhanced with a sense of remoteness and adventure, demanding outdoor skills of the trekkers who cross the range.

The largest and most prosperous Greek island, Crete has several thriving towns, but no big cities, an agreeable Mediterranean climate, an economy based on agriculture as well as tourism and good home-produced food. Crete is easy to reach – dozens of charter flights from the UK and other European countries serve Chania and Heraklion airports.

CHAPTER 1

PRACTICAL INFORMATION

GETTING TO CRETE

There are two main ways of getting to Crete: a flight to Athens (then an internal flight or overnight ferry) or a direct flight to Crete.

Flying to Athens

There are many airlines operating flights to Athens. However, there are advantages in using the Greek airline, Olympic Airways (OA), for ease in continuing the journey to Crete.

Olympic Airways (OA) international flights use their own terminal on the south side of Athens airport. Departing from the UK (or elsewhere) luggage can be consigned right through to Chania or Heraklion airports on Crete.

Other international and charter airlines use the north side of Athens airport.

In case your internal connection is not immediate, pack your in-flight bag to suit this eventuality. In the Olympic Airways south terminal there is a left-luggage office and OA restaurant opposite the Arrivals exit. In the North Terminal (locally called 'charter flights') a left-luggage facility operates outside the terminal (enquire).

Continuing your journey by air or sea

By air. OA internal flights leave from the OA terminal. If you have arrived by the North Terminal transfer around to the OA terminal by No. 019 bus or by taxi. Alternatively, an internal charter flight service may operate from the North Terminal (enquire). For changeovers, charter to OA, allow a minimum of 2 hours from your main flight arrival time (and hope for no delays).

By sea (see Ferry Services below). Ferries leave from Piraeus (port of Athens). To get to Piraeus, either take a No. 019 bus from the OA terminal (from the Arrivals exit turn right for the bus stop) or the North Terminal, or a taxi – fares are metered and comparatively inexpensive. Taxis take up to four passengers. Extra is charged for luggage.

An alternative way of getting to Piraeus from the North Terminal would be to take the airport bus to the centre of Athens (to and from the south side of Syntagma Square). A walk through the Plaka District below the Acropolis will take you to Monastiraki or Thession Metro stations, from where you can get the subway to Piraeus harbour (terminus). If you have time to visit the Acropolis, it would be simplest to take a taxi from the airport and then walk down to the Plaka and the subway stations.

Arriving at Chania
At all internal airports an OA bus service meets OA arrivals. At Chania Airport (tickets sold in Arrivals hall) this bus leaves from the eastern exit of the terminal for the 20 minute run to Chania OA office, where it is fairly easy to get a taxi. For return journeys, the OA bus leaves the Chania OA office 1 hour 50 minutes before flight departures.

Ferry services
From Piraeus, overnight ferries serve the main towns of Crete. Vessels on the Souda ('Soo-tha' – port of Chania) service are the 'Lato' and the 'Lissos'. Alternating, they depart year-round every night from Piraeus (and Souda) at 20.00 and arrive at 06.00 (weather permitting).

In Piraeus they dock in the north corner of the ferryboats' harbour, 10 minutes walk from Piraeus Metro station (Athens city subway) – cross the road and walk north-west along the dockside. Also, the Souda dock is 3 minutes from Piraeus OSE station (Greek National Railway), a small neo-classical building just outside the dock gate. Ask taxi drivers for 'ferryboat to Kreety, Soo-tha' or Piraeus OSE station 'Pee-ray-us Oh-SAY'.

Tickets are sold at agents' offices along the harbour front or at the ship's day-office, which is up the entrance gangway. You can make cabin reservations and board the vessel at any time during the day up to sailing time.

Cabin accommodation includes shower facilities. Deck class (reclining seats) does not. After sailing time, lying down is permitted in certain hallways and on deck. There are restaurants and bars. The cheapest fare (deck class) is about £21 return.

Direct Flights

There are direct flights to Chania and Heraklion airports. At Chania airport, charter flights are met by package tour operators' buses only – take a taxi (metered). Correct fares are listed above the taxi rank (see section on Taxis under public transport below). At Heraklion airport take a 7 minute taxi ride (metered) to the KTEL bus station to catch a bus to Chania. Buses leave every half-hour up to 20.30 for the 2.5 hour journey, via Rethymnon. Alternatively, taxi drivers are eager to get this job as there is a good main road all the way. The fare is about £40.00. The Greek for 'slow down, please' is 'see-gah, parraker LOW'!

GETTING TO THE TRAILHEAD

Public Transport

KTEL (referred to in Crete as 'K'tel'), the Greek public bus organisation, operates an extensive network nationwide. KTEL buses are cream and turquoise – learn to recognise them because there are lots of *touristico* private tour buses, which look similar from a distance. Chania ('Han-YA') bus station (B) is just a few minutes' walk from all other places useful to visitors. There is an authentic, but unglamorous, bus station restaurant. The left luggage store opens between 07.00 and 20.00. Tickets are sold inside the hall or on the bus and seats on busy runs can be pre-booked. The only return ticket issued is the KTEL special for the Samaria Gorge round excursion. English is widely spoken. Town bus stations have information kiosks. Departures are announced in Greek and English and each bus has an individual number on its front window (eg. 'Heraklion – Bus no.78').

Only small daysacks are allowed inside the bus. Other luggage is put in the hold. Tell the conductor your destination as you load it. Carry your valuables inside the bus and (as with air travel) remove 'novelty' items, like karabiners, from you rucksack. Serious thefts occasionally occur at bus stations. Expensive rucksacks are coveted by certain other travellers, so keep an eye on the hold until it is closed for departure. Monitor the unloading of bags at busy bus stops en route, especially when the hold is full – innocent mistakes do occur. It is useful to note the conditions of your insurance concerning luggage in transit. As a rule losses of any kind must be reported to the relevant local

Bringing equipment down from the Madares at the end of the summer

police station within 24 hours, a procedure that is inevitably time consuming.

From the north coast main road that links Heraklion, Rethymnon, Chania and Kastelli other roads branch south over the mountains. In western Crete an important road junction is at Vrises ('Vree-siss') – for here is the road to Hora Sfakion and the south coast. Vrises bus station proprietor, who runs a *bar-kafeneon*, is helpful to tourists. Expect the Chania to Hora Sfakion buses to arrive in Vrises 40 minutes after departing from Chania. Vrises supermarket is open on Sundays.

School Bus and Villagers' Shopping Transport
Services doubling as school buses operate from Chania bus station, rather than from specific villages. Typically, a village bus departs from Chania about 06.00 and then departs from the village at about 07.00 – and repeats that run early afternoon. During school holidays a different service may operate. Ask at the information kiosk for services to villages not listed on the main board. These are community buses so allow 5 minutes either side of stated timetables. On all runs, note Saturday and Sunday variations. Schedules expand with the tourist season, when there are many more passengers.

15

All-year-round Main Bus Routes
These routes are particularly useful to walkers.

Chania to Hora Sfakion and Anopolis
(Note Hora Sfakion is called 'Sfakia' locally.)
Daily, except Orthodox Easter Sunday. Departs Chania at 14.00 and, going via Vrises, serves Askyfou, Imbros, Hora Sfakion (on the south coast) and terminates at Anopolis at about 17.00. This bus returns from Anopolis in the early morning (see the Anopolis section, page 113) and arrives at Chania bus station by 09.15. Depending on the season, other buses to the south coast depart at 08.30 and 11.00 and return in the afternoon and early evening.

Chania to Souyia
Departs at 08.30 and 13.30 for the 2 hour journey to Souyia (passing Ay. Irini Gorge trailhead) and returns at 07.00 and 15.30. Sundays are slightly different. In the tourist season, at Seli Pass ('sell-LEE') (see Walk 8) the Souyia to Chania bus, which departs at 07.00, connects with a bus to Xyloscala, for the Samaria Gorge.

Chania to Omalos and Xyloscala
This run needs special attention: an all-year village service to Lakki (on the Omalos road) terminates there outside the tourist season, when the Samaria Gorge is closed. However, when the gorge is being prepared for opening on the 1 May a skeleton service serves Xyloscala (see the Omalos section, page 47). The schedule expands when the gorge is busy. Check the timetable (including return times) in advance at Chania bus station: people working on the plateau are uncertain of the changing timetable. KTEL buses pass through Omalos hamlet on the way to and from Xyloscala, which are 3 kilometres (1.8 miles) apart, but not all drivers will stop there to pick up passengers. As a result, some Omalos proprietors have a 'trailhead' mini-bus service for their guests. KTEL operates a round-tour ticket for the Samaria Gorge excursion that covers Chania to Xyloscala and Hora Sfakion to Chania. The boat transfer Ay. Roumeli to Hora Sfakion is separate (purchase tickets at Ay. Roumeli). On a one-day trip get this ticket, with its reserved seat from Hora Sfakion and, during busy periods, buy it the night before. The KTEL round could give you more time in the gorge than an organised tour, but this depends on the boat schedule from Ay. Roumeli, which also varies

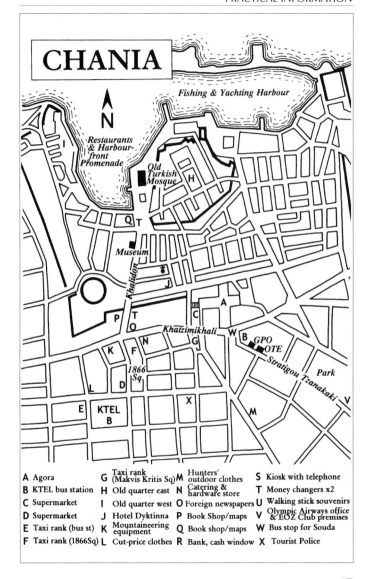

CHANIA

↑
N

Fishing & Yachting Harbour

Restaurants & Harbour-front Promenade

Old Turkish Mosque

Museum

Khaidon

Khatzimikhali

GPO
OTE

Stratigou Tzanakaki

Park

1866 Sq.

KTEL B

A Agora	**G** Taxi rank (Makvis Kritis Sq)	**M** Hunters' outdoor clothes	**S** Kiosk with telephone
B KTEL bus station	**H** Old quarter east	**N** Catering & hardware store	**T** Money changers x2
C Supermarket	**I** Old quarter west	**O** Foreign newspapers	**U** Walking stick souvenirs
D Supermarket	**J** Hotel Dyktinna	**P** Book Shop/maps	**V** Olympic Airways office & EOZ Club premises
E Taxi rank (bus st)	**K** Mountaineering equipment	**Q** Book shop/maps	**W** Bus stop for Souda
F Taxi rank (1866Sq)	**L** Cut-price clothes	**R** Bank, cash window	**X** Tourist Police

according to demand. Eliminate these pressures by staying overnight in Ay. Roumeli if you can (Walk 2). The first boat leaves Ay. Roumeli for Hora Sfakion about noon (50 minutes).

Taxis

Taxis are metered according to a regulated charge per kilometre, which is reviewed annually. Extra is chargeable for luggage and up to four passengers are allowed (certain taxis hold seven passengers). For a party of four, long distance taxi transfers are very economical. It costs about £7 from Chania airport (on the Akrotiri Peninsular) for the 20 minutes journey to town. Taxi drivers dread unmade roads for their dust and winding mountain roads need extra effort. Some drivers may avoid these jobs. Mr. Roussos (Tel. 0821 71113 or 94300) is accustomed to walkers' needs in relation to remote trailheads and advance luggage transfers. If your transport instructions are very detailed, find a bilingual person to help you explain them.

Taxi ranks: Chania airport, Chania bus station exit west side (E), Plateia 1866 east side (F), Plateia Makris Kritis west side (G). In the countryside, if you arrange a lift in a private vehicle, expect the driver to drop you just outside your destination, so that local taxi drivers are not offended.

The Language Barrier

Like all Greeks, Cretans communicate easily with foreigners. Older people involved in tourism learn foreign words and phrases by ear. Nowadays English is taught in school and formal language-learning is left to the young. Also, there are many returnee emigrants from USA, Canada and Australia. For travellers, what really matters are prices. Everyone is used to writing down price totals for tourists. To avoid any misunderstandings carry a notebook and pen for this purpose. Almost all place names are written in Greek and English. A small dictionary is useful (see Books section below).

ACCOMMODATION AND SHOPPING

Chania (see map on page 17)

Flights may arrive after the last KTEL buses to trailhead destinations have left and after Chania shops have closed. Immediate taxi transfers to the countryside save holiday time, but mountain trekkers and campers arriving late will need to bring Greek money with them and start from villages that have supermarkets (see relevant route notes) or bring their own food supplies. Accommodation in mountain villages closes up at about 22.00. From the airport, allow 1.5 hours for journeys to Omalos or Askyfou, and 2.5 hours to Anopolis.

Accommodation
Hotels tend to be block-booked by package tour operators. However, the mid-grade, fairly large Hotel Dictina (J), Tel. 0821 51103, has night staff and unreserved rooms are normally available (ask for rooms facing south as this is the quieter side of the hotel). It is conveniently located in the pedestrian precinct, central to everything useful and attracts local business clients and passing travellers. Rooming houses near the bus station may hire messengers to promote them (not aggressively) to travellers. Of the accommodation near the waterfront, rooms near the cathedral (clock) and east of the harbour (H) are cheaper than those in the (restored) old quarter to the west of it (I). There are dozens of restaurants, coffee bars and fast food places on the waterfront and around the harbour area.

Shopping
Note midday closing, three late-night shopping days and two early-closing days: Tuesday, Thursday and Friday: 08.30–13.30 and 17.00–20.00; Monday and Wednesday: 08.30–13.30; Saturday: 08.30–15.00. On Sundays, except for the fruit and vegetable stall at the bus station, only patisseries and tourist shops are open. All food supplies are available in the Agora (A) and the supermarket opposite its west-facing entrance (C). Very convenient to the bus station is a well-stocked supermarket (D) on the west side of Plateia 1866. Karistiyannis, the mountaineering equipment shop (K), is in Skalidi Street, one block west of Plateia 1866. The owner, Christos (who speaks Greek only), is active in the Chania Alpine Association (EOZ), which organises weekend trips (all over Greece) once a month. An end-of-range clothing shop can be found opposite the north entrance to the bus station (L). A hunters' outfitters is in Apokoronou Street (M). A household goods store for utensils and stoves is in Hadjimichaeli Street (N), first block east of Plateia 1866. A foreign newspapers stall and second-hand bookshop is on the corner (O). Maps and books (P,

Q) and several money changers operate in Halidon Street (T). The National Bank of Greece, opposite the Agora, has a cash dispenser (R) and the GPO and OTE (public telephones) are nearby in Janakaki Street where the OA office and the EOZ club premises (V) can also be found. Many street kiosks have no-fuss (world-wide) telephones on a meter (S) and sell stamps – postal charges are similar throughout the EU. Walking sticks or *katsounas*, shepherds' crooks, traditional to Sfakia, are on sale (£6–£10) in souvenir shops in or just off Halidon Street (U). When choosing one, turn it upside down to check the length from the handle – even if cut down, it should be a minimum of 5cm (2ins) above the waist to be useful on descents.

The Countryside

Thanks to the traffic, two-stroke engines, discotheques, revellers, and pre-dawn garbage collections, much of Chania is very noisy at night. Most south coast and mountain villages are free of church clocks and traffic noise ceases quite early. However, this will probably be replaced by a cacophony of barking dogs, crowing roosters and, in the autumn, chain saws by day. But also, after dark as you have dinner, you will hear the call of a scops owl or a nightingale and, just beyond the nearest street lamp, you will see an open, starry sky before you turn in.

The loss of tranquillity due to the faster pace of life is fully recognised by Cretans. Camping out in the Madares, backpackers may think they have solved it, but as sheep graze after dark when it is cool, flocks can pass back and forth all night, ringing their bells. To be sure of the rare luxury of silence, aim for the Madares in the Spring before the sheep arrive, or for high desert areas beyond Livada after that (Treks 1, 2, 3). Accommodation-based walkers will find Omalos hamlet, a tourist-specific settlement on a cul-de-sac, the quietest place in the mountains (by the afternoon when Samaria Gorge tour buses will have gone).

Accommodation

All tourist accommodation is inspected, graded and price-regulated by the Ministry of Tourism. Proprietors are permitted to drop a price grade at their discretion. Discounts for large groups may apply and rates are reduced if you stay more than one night. Apart from the Chania and Vrises-orientated northern foothills, all the walking centres featured in this guide have family-run lodging houses ('rooms') or hotels (or both) with en suite accommodation and hot water, so long as sunshine heats rooftop solar panels (Omalos hotels switch to alternative power). Walkers on a continuous route can be free of having to make reservations, because it is unlikely that all village accommodation will be full at any one time. There might be a problem in the high season in the resorts of Hora Sfakion and Loutro, in which case you would transfer to Ay. Roumeli, or up to Anopolis or Askyfou (where it is cooler). Omalos' hotels could be full on certain days of the week with group bookings, but the hamlet also has rooming houses. If a place does not do meals, there is always somewhere nearby which does.

In Askyfou and Anopolis, where customer turnover is not continuous, landladies do simple home-cooked meals to order. The choice will be limited, but the food will be wholesome – eat what is on offer. Travelling food vans supply villages with fresh produce to supplement what is home grown. Order chick peas, beans or lentils in advance, but spaghetti and cheese or omelette and pork grills with chips are almost always available. Salad, fruit and vegetables vary in availability. Home-made wine is locally preferred, but if none other is available, your own wine bought elsewhere would not offend in an informal village taverna (but ask). Sheep's milk yoghurt (all milk is boiled) is made in the spring. Breakfast (not included except at Omalos) will be bread and jam, tea or coffee, or 'mountain tea' (made from local herbs). Fresh orange juice, commercially made yoghurt, eggs and local honey might also be available.

Mountain refuges. Other than Kallergi (Walk 4), which is run as a commercial enterprise, Mountain refuges are operated by the Hellenic Alpine Association (EOZ) Chania branch, Tel. 0821 44647. They are unwardened, but kitted out with bunks, mattresses, blankets (take a sheet liner), kitchens (bottled gas), washrooms and wood stoves, so that they have to be kept locked. Hunters shoot the locks off at times (partly to see what is inside), in which case passers-by have access until a work party can do repairs. Make advance arrangements for overnight stays with the EOZ. Club premises, in the basement of the same block as the Olympic Airways office building (21) opposite the park, are opened in the evening on weekdays at 21.00 by club members, some of whom speak English. Closing time varies – arrive, or telephone, before 22.00. The refuges are Volikas (Walk 12, Trek 2), Katsiveli (see Mountain Treks 4, 5 and 6) and Niato (Walk 27).

Shopping
Village shops and supermarkets are open all week, but bakers close on Sundays. Hora Sfakion district has several bakeries, which together supply the busy south coast with its massive daily needs. The boat service transports fresh food supplies daily from Hora Sfakion to Loutro and Ay. Roumeli. Currently (1998) there is no pharmacy anywhere in Sfakia district, but village supermarkets stock basic essentials.

Public Holidays
Orthodox Easter weekend (April or May, dates vary each year) is the most important holiday in Greece. All public transport is crowded as people visit relatives around the country. Other holidays include Independence Day on 25 March (parades in the towns) and 1 May, 15 August, 28 October. Main bus services still operate and tourist shops and village shops will be open.

GENERAL INFORMATION, SKILLS AND EQUIPMENT

Time Differences
Greece is on Eastern European Time: in summer, GMT plus 3 hours and in winter, GMT plus 2 hours.

Lost Luggage
What really matters are your boots and socks – always travel with them on the plane. If you have to replace lost items, Chania has a mountaineering equipment shop and there are other shops (see Chania, Shopping, page 19).

Weather
During spring and autumn, periods of seasonal change, the weather is unsettled. From April up to mid-June it could be cold and wet, fresh and sunny, or warm, overcast and humid – all within the space of ten days. In the autumn, fairly warm temperatures prevail through to November, even when it rains. After mid-June temperatures warm up considerably and sometimes last through to mid-October. In summer, daytime

temperatures of 28-33 °C (80-90 °F) are normal and heatwaves sometimes reach 40 °C (104 °F).

Heatwaves are very difficult – even just before dawn there is little respite. The mountains get breezes – plan high-level walks (perhaps not Walk 40) and long midday breaks. On the south coast the Samaria Gorge river estuary beside Ay. Roumeli offers sea breezes and shady pine trees and, in a good year, freshwater bathing. The KTEL Anopolis/Chania bus departs at 6.30am for Hora Sfakion allowing you to spend part of the day on the coast, travelling by boat, before returning to high level (for overnight) in the late afternoon. Alternatively walk down to Loutro at dawn and return by boat and bus (seldom crowded) to Anopolis in the afternoon. Look out for accommodation with rooms (and balconies) orientated east/west, rather than south.

Rain. December, January, February are rated the wettest months, but 3 day periods of rain, and snow blizzards above 1000 metres, may occur as late as mid-June. At summer's end the hot weather breaks in stages and, after bursts of rain, fine weather returns making October a good month for walking as the heat has gone. Daylight hours are fewer, but sufficient for a good day out. Snow may cover the mountains from the end of November. The thaw will be well advanced by mid-April.

Winds. Crete lies in the path of various winds that can change the weather in half a day. If a long-lasting warm south wind in the spring thaws the snow too fast, quite spectacular natural erosion occurs in the gorges. The mountains attract fierce storms, even in summer. Strong billowing gusts hit below the knee and toss you over. Do as the locals do – wait out the storm; it should ease in half a day. Alternatively, in summer, ordinary north-westerlies cool the mountains, making trekking routes and summit ascents more attractive than low-level walks.

Mist. When the Sirocco – the warm south wind – reaches mountains recently cooled by a north wind, or vice versa, a period of up to three days of mist and rain may follow. (The northern slopes are more prone to mist.) In the high mountains, always assess the next day's route and the whereabouts of the next shelter and water source. From June to October shepherds' huts may be in use. Some shepherds are more sociable and welcoming than others, but all would make space in bad weather.

Photography

Greece is famous for the quality of its light. Photographically speaking, there is 'light in the shadows'. However, there are variations to this: light is crisp and contrasty early in the year, but in summer a haze develops. In the autumn, as if compensating for the absence of greenery, the haze clears and mellows attractively, offering a wider exposure latitude. The Madares (see Mountain Treks, page 143) look their best at this time, but shadows are denser at high altitude. In general, soft early morning light is gone by 8.30am but evenings, after 6.00pm, offer more scope.

Water

In and around the White Mountains, towns and villages are supplied with good water from underground sources. Tap water is normally safe to drink, although it may come via a rooftop tank rather than the mains supply. Chania's supply is chlorinated. Bottled water is widely available.

In the high mountains, after the thaw, nothing is more important than the whereabouts of cisterns and springs. Learning how to find and take care of this water are useful skills to develop. In addition, when it rains you may be able to collect a litre or two on a waterproof sheet, which may help if you are delayed by mist.

Many very old well shafts and cisterns still function throughout Crete despite earth tremors and other ravages of time, thanks to the specialist skills of those who made them. Old cisterns may be topped with stone barrel-vaulting (or just a wooden log) blending so well into the surroundings that you may even miss the whole thing as you pass by. This type is often sited on small flat plains of alluvial soil (dolines), which provide a run-off for rain and snow-melt. Modern cisterns are of reinforced concrete with or without a cover (which may be locked) and the latest are large concrete-aproned constructions, blasted into the hillsides.

Drawing up the water. In these limestone mountains always carry 5 metres of lightweight nylon line and, ideally, a camping pan that doubles as a bucket. Remove your sunglasses or spectacles to a safe place (never on the ground – someone will step on them) and secure the line to your hand or foot before you

Yanni Athitaki, the shepherd of Kolokithas (Mountain Trek 1)

drop the bucket – especially if you are using the shepherds' bucket. Some cisterns are very deep and it may be impossible to retrieve anything dropped in (a large fish hook, obtainable in coastal resorts, could be your only chance). Up-end the bucket and let it drop down square on – to hit the water face down. It should then collect water as it sinks. If it does not, try again. Shepherds have the better knack of raising water without dropping the bucket face down, but this takes practice. If you use the shepherds' bucket, do not allow it to overfill unless you can raise this heavy weight easily – this is not the moment to wrench your back. If you do not have a bucket, form one by putting a plastic-bag-wrapped stone into a carrier bag and, using your length of line, lower this down the well.

Water can be strained through a neckerchief, then filtered, or boiled, or drunk straight off – use your own judgement. However, as recreational use increases, inevitably the danger of giardiasis will apply here as elsewhere in the world. Droppings from (chemically treated) sheep may be around the collection area. Some water is clear and tastes good; some tastes awful. Vegetation near the cistern may have unattractively coloured the run-off, but water of any sort is precious. Replace the logs, or other devices, put there to stop animals from falling in and re-secure the shepherds' bucket if you have used it. Buckets are tied up as strong winds can occur at any time.

Be careful not to contaminate or waste any water. If supplies dry out too soon flocks must be taken down to be fed on (stinted) supplies of purchased fodder. Lastly, if a water trough is empty it may be right for you replenish it. Goats will let you know when they want water more readily than sheep. They emerge from the shade and look at you with big, pleading eyes – you were just leaving, but there you will be landed with filling the trough!

Shepherds may call any sort of water supply simply *nero* so that you may not know whether to look out for a well, a cistern or a spring. They will warn you by saying 'then eenay kal-LOW' ('it isn't good') if it is only fit for animals (without boiling).

Some useful words:

- cistern – *sterna*
- seepage well – 'pig-GAR-thee'
- river – 'pot-AR-mee'
- spring – 'vree-see'

26

- stream – 'ree-ak-ee'
- water – 'ner-RO'
- diminutive for drinking water – 'ner-raki'.

Water allowance. In hot weather and on backpacking treks make a point of replenishing your body reservoir, like a camel, before you set off. Start drinking water, or other liquids, from the time you get up. Supplement your morning tea or coffee with glasses of water. During the day, top up your body reservoir with 100ml gulps, rather than small sips to alleviate a dry mouth. If this is a problem, suck a small (smooth) fruit stone or similar to keep the saliva in your mouth.

Backpackers especially need to rehydrate in the evening: for an overnight camp between water sources, allow an absolute minimum of three litres per person. This has to cover dinner, breakfast, hot drinks, ordinary drinking, teeth-cleaning and minimal washing, so there will not be much left for your start next morning. Plan to stop at the next water source for a big brew up. Along with your water supply, plan your food. For example, a staple like pasta needs more water (and gas cylinder time) for cooking than couscous. In remote places aim to keep 1 litre of water in reserve in case of mishaps or delays. If you are short of water do not eat as this draws on body moisture reserves – being hydrated is much more important than being well fed. Plan gas cylinders to cover daytime brew ups as well as cooking.

Shelter

Shepherds' huts, or *mitatos*, feature throughout the Madares. Made of drystone walling and corbelling, these workstation complexes look like piles of rocks in the landscape, or on the skyline, as several are located over views of the trail. Some *mitatos* are still used during the grazing season (from about mid-June to mid-October) but off-season, having no desirable possessions inside, just old tools, old clothes and perhaps old food, they are left unlocked in case passers-by need shelter. Interiors are normally a mess, but they can be cleaned up. Disused *mitatos* may be structurally unsound; approach these interiors with care. *Mitatos* are usually (but not always) near a water supply.

Caves. Surprisingly for a limestone range, there are not many accessible caves for shelter. Those that do exist are much used by sheep and goats eager for shade.

Types of Pathways

Wherever possible, walks in this guide follow footpaths or mule tracks, rather than roads. 'Underfoot' types are as follows:

Cobbled mule tracks

In their heyday during the Turkish occupation (1669-1898) these *kalderimia* served villages, terracing and grazing pastures. Nowadays these old trails, which so delightfully followed the lie of the land, are in a broken-up state. Sections that had gradients suitable for vehicles have often been entirely replaced by new roads. This policy spares mule tracks up steep ravines, or crags (eg. Walks 12, 37 and 44), but these are subject to ongoing weather erosion. In the two places where mule tracks are still in regular use, and therefore in need of repair (Walks 39 and Trek 7), locations are too remote to attract skilled stonemasons. However, Sellouda might eventually qualify, as at present it remains a valuable optional link between Ay. Roumeli and Anopolis.

Unsurfaced shepherds' roads

These link shepherding villages to traditional grazing pastures in the mountains. They allow shepherds a modern way of life – that is, instead of staying up in the mountains for long periods, especially during the milking season, shepherds are able to drive up in the early morning and bring down the day's milk yield to the village dairy in the evening. As the White Mountains do not have national park status it would be realistic to assume that road cutting will be ongoing, in line with EU funding for this type of development. At present, roads under construction, bit by bit, are designed to access the main high-level grazing pastures around Katsiveli and Potamos (Treks 8 and 6) and to provide a link to the Omalos plateau, and also a branch to meet the Theriso shepherds' route (Trek 1). Livada (Treks 1, 2 and 3) is likely to be targeted next – and then with any luck, there may be a lull. Many Cretans, aware of several beach areas already 'spoiled', do not agree with the shepherds' vote on this matter. The Lefka Ori central massif, with its tough terrain and almost circular shape, is the last wilderness area in Greece to be crossed by a road.

Unsurfaced village link roads

These roads qualify for asphalting before the shepherds' roads. As each is finished, taxi drivers are willing to use them – but walkers will want to find some other route. In Sfakia, judging by the 1950s Hora Sfakion and Anopolis roads, a newly cut road takes about 50 years to blend into the landscape. In places where the rainfall is higher this process is faster.

Footpaths
These are footpaths habitually used by local or recreational walkers, as well as animals.

Goat paths
These are small paths made by sheep and goats. They may be unsafe for walkers.

Splintered paths
As flocks of sheep and goats pass up and down the mountainsides, they form 'splintered' paths, or they may reduce a main footpath into several small paths.

Walking Technique
Footpaths in Crete are endlessly rocky, obliging you to concentrate almost at every step. Tripping up, you will probably land on a thorn bush, or rocks. Have patience with the situation: adjust your walking style – learn to lift your feet and consciously discipline yourself to slow down immediately you notice yourself stumbling. It may be galling if your companions are faster than you, but accept this, and stick to your own safe pace. In this way you will be a competent walker. Shepherds use *katsounas* (long sticks) in the mountains. Buy one or bring a trekking pole (see Chania Shopping, page 19).

Exploring. Weather erosion has reduced many old footpaths, unmaintained for decades, to a dangerous or even non-existent state. Even in the busy Samaria Gorge some (forbidden) side trails are so unfrequented that you would be in trouble if you got into difficulties there – be careful.

Rock Scrambling. The walks in this guide do not involve rock scrambling unless this is mentioned, but as a reminder the basic rules are: do not explore DOWN unless you are absolutely sure you can get back up again, and do not explore UP unless you can get down again. Rock scrambling (unroped) is the most dangerous form of mountaineering.

The E4 Trail
This is the European long distance walking Route No.4 that starts

in Spain and ends on Crete's eastern shore at the Minoan Palace of Zakros (archaeological site). In Greece the E4 Trail (the *Epsilon Tessera*) is all too often routed along roads more stimulating to mountain bikers than to walkers. However, some footpath sections are a delight. In Crete the E4 Trail starts at Kastelli and takes in several of the less-visited archaeological sites on its journey east. Cretan branches of the Hellenic Alpine Association (EOZ) have designated several E4 Trail branch options: coast and mountains (see contour maps).

The E4 Trail is waymarked with aluminium yellow and black poles ('parking meters') supplemented in places with the paint-marked rocks the EOZ would have preferred. Winter storms strip the poles, shotgun owners use them as targets and souvenir hunters remove the flag signs. Positioning trail markers needs a practised understanding of sight lines, and of other people's thought processes so that getting it exactly right as a one-off job is difficult. Therefore, overall, relying on the poles to show you the way can be stressful and frustrating. Instead, do not be deskilled by the E4 Trail – take time to consider the lie of the land, looking for likely footpaths, as you would be doing if it did not exist. When it appears, a marker will then come as useful confirmation that you have got it right.

Turkish fort above Ay. Roumeli (Walk 47)

Backpacking and Camping

Sleeping bags. Many lodging houses have easy-care nylon blankets that are hardly warm enough in the spring. To meet this problem, bring thermal underwear. Similarly, for indoor use, a one-season sleeping bag or a warm liner is a welcome but not essential luxury. For camping in the mountains, a zipped three-season bag is the good all-rounder. However, from July to September, a one-season bag may suit even at altitude, especially if it is upgraded with a Gortex 'bivi' bag. In the warmer months nylon materials are uncomfortable: bring a cotton or silk inner liner (which is also useful against insects).

Mattresses. Lightest and most comfortable of the insulation mats are Cascade Designs' Z-Rest and Ridgerest. Self-inflatables are greatly at risk from thorns and thistles. Protect your expensive mattress with a piece of tough polythene DPM (damp-proof membrane) undersheet (builders' supplies). This also works as a shower and washing mat and, supported with rocks, makes a bowl for clothes-washing, for you must not contaminate any water trough with soap.

Tents. In rocky terrain, the more self-supporting your tent type is, the more convenient it is likely to be.

'Bivi' bags. On two-day treks – one overnight out – a non-breathable polythene survival bag will do. On longer-range treks you need a breathable 'bivi' bag. Camping with a 'bivi' bag in the rain is not easy; an umbrella is useful. You will see a squalid *mitato* interior, or cave, in a new light if mist and rain sets in for three days.

Cooking stoves. Small gas stoves that take the fixed, non-valved 190g gas cylinder are popular throughout Greece. Greek manufactured cylinders are available in remote places and Camping Gaz C206 supplies are available in towns. Therefore, this type of stove is best for Crete. Note that valved (removable and resealable) gas cylinders are not available and also that you cannot take gas cylinders (or liquid fuel of any sort) on an aircraft because, as manufacturers readily confirm, air pressure might cause seals to open and release the highly combustible liquid gas. 190g gas cylinders are reckoned to last for about 2.5 hours, but this depends on conditions – use a windshield (aluminium foil). Three slim-profile stoves grouped together are good for melting snow in a large pan. The Camping Gaz C206 stove head needs checking for tightness each time before it is lit. Practise cylinder changing in advance. Carry a 'last resort' set of matches encased with their striker in a reliably waterproof container, like a plastic medicine bottle.

Cooking pans. Wherever drinking water has to be boiled or filtered, or carried from source, a cooking pan of a minimum of 1 litre capacity is an essential tool. For the cisterns, your own bucket is pleasant to have, and for this, the old-fashioned loop-handled billy has never been bettered, but this is now hard to find. A (disposable) billy can be made out of a large food can (supermarkets) and wire and lightweight two-handle pans can be bought in Chania (see Chania Shopping, page 19).

Rucksacks. In summer, backpackers might avoid alpinists' sacks, which are designed to fit close to the back. If you are caught in a storm without a waterproof liner, use your 'bivi' bag for this job.

Litter. Greece is no stranger to marketing devices, and there is an abundance of product packaging. As recreational walkers, set an example – bring all your rubbish out of the mountains and countryside. Women, note that buried sanitary materials are dug up by animals. Most villages are supplied with large rubbish trolleys and villagers recognise the problem, even if visiting Cretan town-dwellers apparently do not. Boat service notices ask passengers not to throw litter into the sea. Win local approval by being seen to put your rubbish in the village bins.

In wilderness situations the loss of any item is inconvenient. After any sort of stop during the day, always look behind you as you leave in case you have forgotten something. Soft cleaning sponges left out overnight may be stolen by animals that live in burrows. Take something to do, or read, so that if thick mist develops you can wait patiently and confidently until it clears.

Water Bottles

On mountain treks, your water bottle for immediate use needs to be 100% reliable. The easy-fill, lid-attached, wide-mouth, easy-clean, transparent, non-tasting, high-impact Lexan 1 litre Nalgene or Coleman water bottle must be the best design yet. Platypus bottles in new condition are good for back-up. Use the simple

cent of Gingilos - heading for the pinnacles, the big scree slope over on the left (Walk 1)

On the shepherd's footpaths to Zourva, Lakki in the distance (Walk 10)

Looking down on Ay. Roumeli from the fort (Walk 47)

The route as seen from Kambi. The two ravines are in view, right, as is Spathi (Walk 12)

screw top. They make hot water bottles at night (your drinking water for next day perhaps) and good cold compresses too. Alternatively, on a budget, use fizzy drinks bottles as these are very tough. (Mineral water bottles may split if dropped.) Protect nylon water bags carefully from thorns and thistles.

Daysack Essentials

In warm temperatures, a framed daysack with an effective hip belt is much more practical than a simple nylon daysack, plastered to the back.

'Daysack essentials' are contingency-plan items that each individual hillwalker should carry in case of sudden changes in the weather, changes of plan, or unfortunate mishaps. Hikers of the Sierra Club of California neatly call this matter 'The Twelve Essentials'. This is their checklist: rainshell clothing, spare warm layer, warm hat, gloves, water bottle, spare food, map, compass, torch, whistle, pocket knife, survival bag. Think this through as: spare clothing, sustenance, navigation aids, means of attracting attention, a minimum of one useful tool and shelter.

In Crete take these contingency items on all summit ascents and mountain walks, because whatever it looks like when you set off, unpredictable winds can bring mist and heavy rain by the evening.

In addition, it would be wise to extend the checklist to include: blister kit, knee and ankle support tubes, polythene bag rucksack liner, sunglasses (your hat counts as an 'everyday' item), sun cream, Greek/English dictionary or vocabulary list. And, for communal use, also carry a 'water' kit (see section on Water above), which comprises: 5 metres of string and a plastic carrier bag, a purification outfit or a brew up kit including matches.

If most 'daysack essentials' seem a fiddly nuisance, parcel them up into one separate, brightly coloured stuff bag and belay this to the inside of your rucksack. Also, attach a belt keyholder clip onto your rucksack and secure your trekking pole wrist-strap to this whenever you are not using it – then you won't leave it behind.

On Grade A and low-level Grade B walks, especially during warmer months, you need less. Your checklist could be: long-sleeved shirt (or rainshell), spare warm layer (thermal vest or T-

*Yanni Papasifis, a shepherd from Anopolis who welcomed
many travellers at Pirou mitato*

shirt in a plastic bag), water bottle, spare food, map, whistle, sunglasses, sun cream, blister kit, knee and ankle support tubes and a pocket knife.

If you plan to use the boat service, or find bus journeys on winding roads unpleasant, you may want to include travel sickness pills.

If you are with a group, do not automatically rely on others – make sure that you understand the itinerary and know the name of your destination. Have your own supply of Greek money with you. Sometimes a series of unlucky coincidences can separate you from your companions.

Blisters and First Aid

Zinc Oxide plaster applied directly to the skin (check before you leave any for allergy) protects against foot burn, rubbing, and chaffing – the skin conditions that precede blisters. Zinc Oxide is removable (with care) overnight. Carry proprietary blister dressings such as Compeed, and your own knee and ankle support tubes (chemists, UK). On the mountain, a get-you-home device is sheep or goats' wool as it makes a resilient padding, but do not put wool next to broken skin. Include a Vick menthol inhaler in your first aid kit in case a thick head cold is going about. Take travel sickness pills in case of a rough crossing if you use the ferry.

Compass and Altimeter
Magnetic declination in Greece is zero. Contour maps are small scale and not detailed, but you can take bearings off identifiable mountain tops, passes or plateaux, and check the direction of valleys, ravines and mule tracks. An altimeter is a useful additional aid. For final route planning, note the daylight hours as soon as you arrive. By the end of October (when clocks go back) there are 10 hours of daylight.

Maps
Several maps available to tourists show contours, footpaths and the E4 Trail. Based on an up-to-date military survey, contours and mountain summits, although small scale, are accurate. All other information varies from map to map. 'Footpaths' may in fact be district boundaries or notional watercourses and new roads may be in the wrong place.

Budget about £7 for a map: a recent series Harms Verlag: 1:80,000 (No.1 Chania) is discontinued in favour of Harms verlag: 1:100,000 (No.1 Western part) 'Touring Map with footpaths and the E4 Trail'. This map is the best readily available (1998). An economically priced map is Efstathiadis: 1:79,000 'with footpaths' (No.1, Chania). A less detailed map is Petrakis ed.1996 scale 1:100,000 'Trekking and Road Map' (No.1, Chania).

Stockists: (UK) Stanfords Ltd, 12-14 Longacre, London WC2 0171 836 1321 or Fax 0171 236 0189. In Chania good maps may sell out by September. Hora Sfakion shops stock the Petrakis edition.

Clothing and Footwear
In spring, autumn and winter bring one outfit of lightweight quick-drying synthetic fabrics. Above a certain level of humidity all synthetics are uncomfortable, so you also need an outfit of cotton such as shorts and T-shirt. Lightweight tight-weave cottons are quick-drying and wind resistant, whilst soft loose-weaves help against chaffing. To travel light, consider the versatility of silk which is quick drying, fairly wind and insect proof, quite warm and yet wearable in the worst humidity.

Underwear. In case of chaffing, pack two different types. If underwear incorporates synthetics, also bring cotton alternatives.

Warm layers. Depending on the season and the altitude, you need one, two or three warm layers from the following range: thermal underwear, a lightweight wool or fleece pullover and a fleece jacket or light duvet. In rooming houses and hotels, facilities for drying clothes are minimal – keep dry clothes in reserve. For this, backpacking trekkers may have to change back into damp clothes, which is why synthetic dry-on-the-body materials are so practical.

Rainshell. Lightweight Gortex is best as it doubles as a windproof. Any waterproof is better than nothing. As storms can occur at any time of year, on mountain treks and summit ascents, however settled it looks, you must have a rainshell. An umbrella is useful. Overtrousers and gaiters are a welcome luxury.

Protective clothing. In summer, wear loose-fitting cottons that protect you from the sun and from chaffing. Check that all clothes are comfortable in use, and bring long sleeved tops and long trousers, which also help against the insect nuisance that builds up over the summer. If the heat is exhausting, use an umbrella – your own pool of shade makes all the difference.

Boots. Wear boots with good ankle and foot-muscle support as the footpaths, with loose stones, and even the service tracks, are relentlessly rough underfoot. Shock absorbing footbeds are particularly helpful in Crete. However, in hot weather you will need generously sized boots and the introduction of either thick insoles or two pairs of socks, or both, could make your boots too tight: check these options when you buy the footbeds. The rough limestone is very abrasive – run a protective film of Super Glue along boot stitching. Ideally your older pair of boots would suit Crete conditions, but they must not fall apart. If this threatens, find Nico the bootmaker in Ammoudari (Askyfou): his work-cabin (open weekdays) is opposite Barba Geronimo's rooms. Undaunted by modern adhesive-dependent designs, he will fix your boots at least so that they will last out the holiday.

Shoes. Velcro-fastening sandals are useful for sea bathing or river crossings. Some cheap varieties are ultra-light.

Socks. In principle two pairs of socks, perhaps one soft loop stitch and one coarse, are best for perspiration-wicking and

On the way down to Ay. Pavlos from Sellouda (Walk 39)

cushioning. Cotton becomes saturated, which causes chaffing. High wool-content socks may work better than the synthetics. Skin that causes no trouble at home may react differently in the heat. On a first venture bring a variety of sock types, including cotton. Long socks you can pull up against thorns are useful if you wear shorts. Canvas gaiters are a luxury especially on northern footpaths – walkers soon appreciate why knee high leather boots are part of the traditional Cretan dress.

Ultra-light clothing alternatives. In the mountains, where storms can occur at any time of year, function-specific clothing is needed in winter, spring and autumn. In summer also, you must have a shell jacket and an effective warm layer, but other minimum weight 'just in case' items could be as follows: sew an elastic chin strap onto your sun hat so that it stays on in a wind and provides warmth. Wear a plastic bag under it (or over it) if it rains. Cotton or silk scarves are useful and versatile: bring at least two. For the hands, latex gloves are windproof. A ring made out of spare socks (toes inside ankles) makes a warm hat. Spare socks can also be used as gloves. Nylon tights make effective long johns. Polythene bags can be formed into boot-top gaiters. As a last resort, a large polythene dustbin bag worn next to the skin, under wet clothes, acts as a vapour barrier, helping to conserve body heat (this is for overnight camp – remove the vapour barrier when you move). Gortex is best for 'bivi' bags, but a better-than-polythene 'bivi' bag can be made of proofed Pertex, available by the metre (see classified adverts in 'outdoor' magazines). For all packing, think carefully about reducing weight as on some routes you may need to carry lots of water at 840gr/2.4lbs per litre.

Emergencies

There is no official mountain rescue service. Expect to pay for local help. Shepherds are best at finding lost people, usually after other search parties have given up. Sfakiot opinion on trekking ventures is 'if you can't handle it, you shouldn't be doing it.' This guide has been written to give you the necessary information, but the message is: **take extra care on all your routes**. Injuring yourself and then running out of water is the chief danger. If you are an EU national keep your National Health Service (NHS) claim form E.111 (obtainable from Post Offices) in your first aid kit. A Tetanus inoculation is advisable.

Keep a *whistle* on your person although it will be ineffective in a wind. Ideally supplement it with a *strobe or flares* or at least a *good quality torch*. Flares are said to be best for attracting attention, but in this rocky mountain range a Skystreme location marker – an inflatable radar reflective kite weighing 1oz (Tel. 01931 71444, UK) or go to the web site on the internet, www.cumbria.com/survival) would have more chance of being spotted by the sharp-eyed shepherds and by a helicopter. A helicopter might see lights if conditions allowed and so might a search party. It would be easier to find your way back to someone in difficult terrain (this problem happens) if they had both lights and a Skystreme.

Mobile phones. These apparently function from the top of Pachnes (1998). Note the telephone number of the Kallergi Refuge (Tel. Chania district 0821 74560) as staff are knowledgeable on rescue operation possibilities. They also operate their own radio communications system.

Leave a note. In Anopolis and Askyfou people know the mountains and are well aware of the risks involved. Before setting off on a mountain trek, you could leave a note of your plans (with dates) in your own language with your rooming house proprietor, or at a central *kafeneon*.

Lone Women Walkers

In Greece there is great respect for the family, and, therefore, the role women play within the family. Cretan, and especially Sfakiot, society is very 'macho', but lone women travellers and walkers are as safe in Crete as anywhere. However, women travelling on their own for pleasure, curiosity or interest should be aware that this could be misconstrued. It is not a normal part of the local culture and neither are the high mountain Madares (a men-only workplace) visited by Sfakiot women.

Cretan women of the countryside have observed visiting foreign women for many years, so they are well aware of what they miss or gain in comparison. In the mountains, meet the culture halfway by creating (if necessary) an impression of community patronage – give the name of an accommodation-destination address: as every family is known. Examples of respected contacts are: in Anopolis – Theodoros and Chrissi Athitaki (The Helvetia, Kambia); in Askyfou/Ammoudari – the Yalidakis family (Barba Geronimo's taverna); in Ay. Roumeli-Andreas Stavroudaki (the 'Tara'); and in Omalos: George Drakoulakis (New Omalos Hotel).

Manners. For both sexes, quiet considerate good manners are noticed and appreciated. Young Cretans tend not to display affection in public.

Foreign Workers

Many thousands of workers from North Africa and Eastern Europe now live temporarily in Greece: even the smallest village may have two or three in residence; a modest cottage, or the old school house, may be turned into a dormitory for them.

In Chania, workers wait in Plateia 1866 each day to be hired according to standard day-rates and conditions laid down by the government. Albanians are largely employed in labour-intensive seasonal agricultural work. Skilled stonemasons from Albania and Rumania find a rich source of work in the limestone areas. Many other construction workers, waiters and shop assistants are from countries other than Albania. Employed to run the Ay. Ioannis-owned taverna at Ay. Pavlos (Walks 45,49) you might find a Moroccan (thoroughly enjoying that idyllic spot) whilst operating a bulldozer might be a Syrian, enthusiastically hoping to settle permanently.

39

In the mountains some shepherding work may be done by non-local men and against this eventuality, see the 'Lone women' section above, as the 'meet the culture' approach might not be applicable. Western Cretans firmly encourage foreign workers to stay out of trouble, but as so many live far from their homes and families, people in the countryside no longer feel as safe as they once did.

Insects

Mosquitoes. These are present from the Spring, especially in low-lying areas. Mountain accommodation is free of them, at least until midsummer. On white walls, they are fairly easily located and swatted. Supermarkets sell anti-mosquito products. Some hotels and rooms issue plug-in devices. Bring a good insect repellent. Micro mosquito nets for travel come with hanging devices suitable for tents rather than hotel rooms. Supplement your kit with additional lightweight line and several pairs of self-adhesive white plastic hooks, pads or clips (from tool shops and ironmongers). Leave the hooks behind; wrenching them off spoils the paint.

Cockroaches. Stepping on a cockroach apparently causes its eggs to disperse in all directions. Shovel it out of the window, hoping the cat will get it, or toss it over on its back and leave room staff to remove it – they will have the practice.

Hornets. These look like large wasps and the locals say their sting is severe. Luckily this insect is not aggressive: be careful not to provoke it.

Wasps, also, do not normally attack.

Fleas and flies. Many footpaths are also sheep's routes and in summer fleas may be in full swing in the shady sections. If there is no breeze *flies*, too, may now spoil picnic sites that, since the spring, have filled up with droppings. Late September, when shepherds have burnt patches of hillside, these areas are newly free of insects (other than ants).

Honeybees. Beehives are located in groups, usually beside shepherds' roads, remote from the villages. Bees are very active in the spring when flowers appear. Worker bees flying about occasionally sting passing walkers. Protect the back of your neck and, if stung (quite rare), locate and remove the shaft immediately as, once in, it continues to dispense venom.

Sea Urchins

Sea urchins are small, round, jet-black spiny creatures that live on rocks near the seashore. If you step on one the spines are almost impossible to extract. You will not be walking anywhere until your body absorbs them, which takes about six months. If in doubt, wear Velcro sandals in the sea.

Dogs

In the countryside dogs are regarded as useful tools for guarding premises or livestock. Their need for affection is ignored. Dogs chained up for most of their lives, sometimes out of sight even of stimulating diversions, quite naturally become demented. Therefore, if you feed these dogs (they usually need it) take care not to get too close, or to turn your back on them, for many (but not all) will bite you if they can. By law, all dogs are inoculated against rabies and other relevant diseases.

Wildlife and Hunting

Privation due to less high-yield agricultural methods, especially after the Second World War, are remembered throughout Greece and 'food for free' of all types is still of great interest to many people. In the countryside various edible wild greens are gathered in the spring. Snails are also collected for food in the spring (and during Lent), especially after rain.

The *agrimi* goat (*kri-kri*) of the Samaria Gorge is seriously protected from hunting. This is accepted by the gorge community, but *kri-kri* leaving the gorge are probably still at risk from shepherds on the lookout for anything to vary their diet. Vultures and eagles are officially protected from hunting, but they, too, are at risk.

The hunting season officially starts mid-September. The standard prey is *chukar* (a type of partridge that nests in rocky terrain above 1,800m/5,905ft) and mountain hare. To the regret of the locals (who hunt) this prey is now quite rare. The Lefka Ori itself is not a National Park: new roads and off-road vehicles exacerbate the situation. You may be asked if you saw hare or heard *chukars* (a chattering chorus in the early morning) on your trek.

A threat to chickens, and killed at any time, are martins and weasels. Hunting dogs kill badgers. There are various rodents,

41

bats, hedgehogs, frogs and harmless lizards. It is quite unusual to see a snake, which would be a variety of European adder. There are small scorpions but they are not a great threat – take care when handling dead firewood.

Plants, Trees and Flowers
Crete's geological history and location in the eastern Mediterranean, equidistant from Europe, Asia and Africa, renders the island of great interest to botanists (see Books below).

Below 1000m, varying between the south (earlier) and the north coasts, on average the first two weeks of May are best for a profusion of spring flowers. In the high mountains carpets of crocii, chionodoxa, Cretan tulip, and others, bloom with the retreating snow. Autumn flowers appear in October, with the first rains of winter.

The most commonly seen plants and trees are largely those that taste bad to goats. Except for the resinous pine forests that are (even naturally) thinned out by forest fires, Cretan plants are adapted in various ways to survive the long dry summers. They may be geophytes (earth-plants) with sustaining bulbs, quorms, or tubers unsuited to well-watered ground, or sclerophylls (hard-leaved) shrubs or trees with long roots and drought-resistant leaves, or thorns. Deep gorges orientated north/south get shade for part of the day and their shear walls are a safe haven for many species of chasmophyte (gorge plants).

The limit of the treeline varies: northern slopes about 1,450m (4,760ft), southern slopes about 1,600m (5,250ft). Common mountain trees are: Cretan Cypress, often contorted by winter winds, but living to a very old age (the Gingilos path, Walk 3), juniper, Evergreen Maple and Prickly Oak (above Askyfou Walks 24, 27) and Calabrian Pine (Anopolis). Mid-level trees include (apart from olive trees) carob with its big black pods (in the ravine above Loutro, Walk 33), wild pear (Walk 12 to Volikas), deciduous oaks (Walks 13, 18 in Apokorona), Oriental Plane (water courses, village squares), Walnut and fast-growing pollarded Mulberry (Imbros and Askyfou). At the seashore, Juniper and Tamarisk (Souyia and Loutro) can be seen. Tamarisk is usefully fast-growing but despised for the windblown dust (that can land on the dinner table) retained by its foliage. Chestnut groves flourish further west, where the type of rock allows a better water supply.

On the hillsides, trees and other plants make up three main types of vegetation:

Maquis. Tall, long-lived, woody shrubs classed as trees. Includes Prickly Oak, which goats eat, when it is chronically stunted by browsing. *Maquis* is kept down where mature trees monopolize the available water supply.

Phrygana ('frigg-an-na'). This includes heathland plants such as Thyme and Spiny Spurge (the wire-netting plant) and (walkers' worst) woody shrubs that do not develop into trees, such as Spiny Broom, Thorny Burnet and Jerusalem Sage. In late summer shepherds burn areas of *phrygana* to promote regeneration of plants palatable to sheep and goats. If this operation is unlucky, or misjudged, high winds spread the fire. On reaching a ridge top, this type of fire should go out, or at worst 'jump' to elsewhere rather than descend the other side of the ridge.

Phrygana in flower causes hay fever in the spring. Pharmacies (Chania) stock a range of drugs for this 'aller-yee-ah' (allergy). Use your neckscarf as a mask particularly when passing Jerusalem Sage. Fortunately goats can at least nibble the pods of this tough plant, which chokes so many old trails.

Steppe. Plants that grow on exposed dry rocky terrain of the south coast escarpment – includes White Asphodel (spring), Maritime Squill (autumn) and the weird-looking Dragon Arum or Stink Lily. Steppe also includes the long-rooted, nutritious (for sheep) low-profile endemics of the Madares. Several species, adapted to the shadeless, barren terrain, date from geo-historical times indicating that the high mountains were never tree-covered.

Around the White Mountains all three of these types grow side by side depending on the conditions of water supply, orientation and altitude. But in the far west (Selino and Kastelli), where the rock is different, impenetrable, tall heather and sclerophylls blanket many hillsides.

CHAPTER 2

ROUTE NOTES

THE GRADING SYSTEM

Each walk is graded. The grading system used is similar to that used in commercial trekking.

Grade A: Short walks, easy underfoot, with hamlets or destinations in sight.

Grade B: Walks on popular, well-tramped, easy-to-follow trails.

Grade C: Walks on less frequented or mountain footpaths.

Grade D: Tough day-walks on remote terrain. Confidence and route-finding experience is needed. Any of the backpacking routes, as these are mini-expeditions that need careful planning. (See Skills section on page 22.)

Grade E: The toughest backpacking routes.

WALKING TIMES

The walking times listed as Time Allowance are based on the average-time easy-to-calculate formula of:15 minutes per 100 metres of height gained and per approximate linear kilometre:15 minutes on roads, 20 minutes on easy-to-follow rough footpaths, 30 minutes on very demanding terrain.

Time allowance for some rocky footpath descents may not be much less than for ascents. A new route always takes longer to walk than one with which you are familiar. E0Z times on E4 Trail signposts are probably matched to the club's strongest walkers who already know the routes.

On all routes allow extra time for any sort of rest stop – picnics, sitting down, taking photographs – a total one hour at least on most walks. Using Walk 28, Ascent of Kastro, as an example, if there are 10 daylight hours, you may have only 1.5 hours to spare for preparation and stops. On some other routes you may need to catch a bus or a boat. Monitor your own pace on your first couple of walks to check if you want to reduce or extend the Time Allowance formula. The kilometre distances are an approximate guide to be read in conjunction with the other data: maps are not sufficiently detailed for accurate measurement and most routes include zigzagging footpaths. For a very quick guide to the effort involved on a walk, divide Time Allowance figure by kilometre distance. For example, the most-tramped footpath in Crete, the Gorge of Samaria, works out at 16.5 minutes per kilometre, while Trek 7a works out at 50 minutes per kilometre, due to the long, steep ascent and care needed on that remote, broken up old track.

POINT TO POINT ROUTE SUGGESTIONS

A good travelling-light walkers' one-week continuous route (after 1 May) including all facilities. Lakki to Omalos, Samaria Gorge, Ay. Roumeli to Loutro or Anopolis, Hora Sfakion and up the Imbros Gorge to Askyfou (Walks 11a, 2, 45 or 49, 42 or 36, 22, 21, 20).

Either a long coastal walk or trek. Hora Sfakion, Loutro, Ay. Roumeli, Souyia, Paleochora (Walks 42, 45, Trek 10). Supplies for Trek 10 at Ay. Roumeli. In the winter months building construction and maintenance in the resorts goes on so that some facilities may stay open. Omalos and Ay. Roumeli people are very knowledgeable about their gorge – take their advice about it in winter. When there is no boat service, they know when it can be safely walked as a through route. It will be most dangerous during the thaw. Do not start up (or down) it unless you are fully prepared to retrace your steps.

A semi-backpack, mid-level route when high mountains are snow-covered. From Souyia up the Ay. Irini Gorge (Note: river in spate at the top during the thaw) to Omalos (Walks 9, 8), then to Zourva (Walk 10). On to Drakona (road tramp) via the Theriso road (start of Trek 1). Continuing to Kambi, and Melidoni (Walk 13), to Fres/Vafes, then Askyfou, or Krappis and Lake Kourna (Walks 18, or 32). Meals at Souyia, Omalos, Zourva, Kambi (*kafeneon*) Melidoni (*kafeneon*), Vafes, Krappis, Askyfou. Supplies at Souyia, Askyfou. Simple supplies at Omalos, Kambi, Melidoni, Vafes. Accommodation at Souyia, Omalos. Simple accommodation at Kambi and Melidoni (ask when you get there).

Wet walking in the Samaria gorge in spring – one of several crossings

A one-week backpacking route (after June) entirely free of roads (1998). Kambi to Livada (Trek 2) then Katsiveli and Potamos (Treks 4, 5). Potamos to Ay. Ioannis (Trek 7), then the Sellouda trail to Ay. Roumeli (Walks 38, 39) and lastly, the coastal path to Souyia (Trek 10). Meals at Kambi and Ay. Ioannis (omelettes and chips), new supplies at Ay. Roumeli.

The toughest backpacking route. This walk goes up the Kallikratis gorge and then to Askyfou via Angathes summit (Walks 26, 24 in reverse). Niato and the E4 Trail to Livada and Katsiveli, Melendaou and Kallergi (Treks 3, 4, 5, 6). Then over the western massif via Strifomadi, to Souyia (Walk 6). Meals at Kallikratis, Askyfou, Kallergi. Supplies at Askyfou, Xyloscala.

CHAPTER 3

MOUNTAIN WALKS

THE OMALOS PLATEAU

Introduction

The Omalos plain (called 'plateau') is 3 kilometres across, the largest of several high plains in the White Mountains. Just beyond the plateau, on the south side, is Xyloscala, the busy trailhead for the walk down through the Samaria Gorge National Park. From Xyloscala, footpaths lead eastwards to the high mountains via Kallergi Refuge, or westwards to the summit of Gingilos, its massive grey cliff forming part of the Samaria Gorge's north-west wall.

At Omalos hamlet and Xyloscala, various establishments, run by people from Lakki village, specialise in providing quick, sustaining breakfasts to the thousands who walk the Samaria Gorge each day. Trekkers leaving for the high mountains should note that the only shop, at Xyloscala, does not stock provisions other than snacks. The New Omalos Hotel (at Omalos hamlet) can normally supply meat, eggs, cheese, tomatoes, fruit and bread. Otherwise bring lightweight food supplies up with you.

Omalos (1,080m/3,545ft) attracts and holds typical mountain weather: rain, mist, winds, frost, and metres of snow in winter. For Cretans who have to work all summer, the hotels with their home cooking and log fires, make this a popular winter weekend destination, especially when snow transforms a formerly parched summer landscape. At other times of year the cool fresh air is a welcome relief from the heat of coastal resorts and a few days' stay is popular with walking groups.

In May people comb the old meadows collecting *stamnagathi*, the highly regarded edible plant of the Cretan mountains. Growing flat to the ground, its spines have to be painstakingly removed before it is boiled for about 20 minutes.

Apart from the asphalted main roads entering from the north

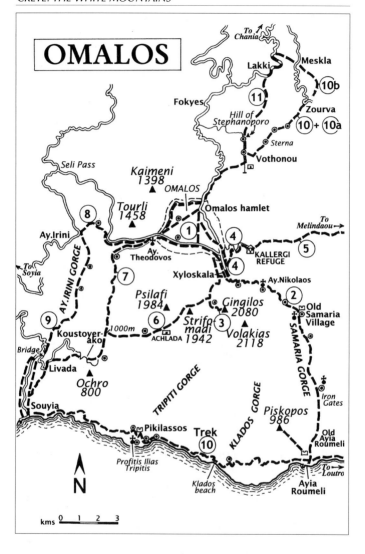

OMALOS

and west, earthen tracks criss-cross the plateau and a gravel road skirts the northern side. A long sink-hole drains snow-melt and rainwater that emerges far below as springs, inland from Chania. Drivers use the earthen service tracks tentatively, aware that a new sink-hole might develop at any moment.

The Toubi *Walkers guide to the Samaria Gorge* is usefully informative on the gorge itself and the Omalos region, but the chapter on other walking routes is interesting rather than practical. For the mountain guiding services suggested in the Toubi publication, contact the Chania Alpine Association (EOZ) in Chania (Tel. 0821 44647).

Walk 1. Around the Plateau

Grade:	A
Time allowance:	Allow 20 minutes per kilometre: straight across the plateau is about 3 kilometres. A return to Omalos hamlet on either of the rim roads (the northern rim road is the shortest) adds 1 or 2 kilometres to the return trip – measure this from your map.

Walkers can avoid the asphalt roads by using sheep paths, the northern rim-road and the service tracks. Patience will be needed with shepherds' fencing and gates. The whole area is heavily grazed, but wild flowers survive here and there, on the borders of the old meadows and around the edge of the plateau. The two-storey, white taverna in the hamlet belonging to Ay. Irini village, just under the western pass, is a popular destination from Omalos hamlet. Economically-priced rooms are provided.

A few of the rare ambelitsia trees, endemic to the Omalos region, grow in the dry watercourse descending from the Strifomadi/Psilafi massif. Ambelitsia is used to make the traditional shepherds' crook of Sfakia. Ruined summer houses ring the edge of the plateau, as this was (and still is) a transhumance destination for shepherds of Ay. Irini and Lakki. Much needed by the busy hotels, cheese is still made here in the spring – excellent mountain-produced *graviera* that does not reach Chania.

Directions
Walk south out of Omalos hamlet and turn right to head west, just past the last taverna, onto an earthen track. For the rim-road, follow the track as it bears right to avoid the main sink-hole. Alternatively, head straight overland to the western taverna, which is in sight, passing south of the sink-hole when you come to it. Either return via the rim-road or follow the asphalt road around the south side, and recross the plateau on any likely-looking service track.

Walk 2. The Gorge of Samaria

See also Walk 46

Grade:	B
Starting point:	Xyloscala (1,250m/4,100ft) – Omalos
Access:	KTEL Omalos bus or taxi from Chania
Finishing point:	Ay. Roumeli
Access:	coastal boat service (see details below)
Approximate distance:	18km (11mls)
Time allowance:	Xyloscala to Ay. Nicolas chapel: 1hr 30mins; to Samaria old village: 1hr 10mins; to Iron Gates: 1hr 10mins; to Park Boundary: 40mins; to Ay. Roumeli waterfront: 30mins. Total 5 hrs.

This hugely popular walk down the Samaria Gorge has brought much prosperity to western Crete. Cretans now recognise that tourists often enjoy shady gorges as well as beaches and several other gorge-walking routes have become popular.

Although the Samaria Gorge has developed in this way, part of it was designated a nature reserve as long ago as 1929 when biologists recognised that the Cretan ibex, or *agrimi* – affectionately called the *kri-kri* – would soon become extinct if they didn't take steps to save it. This ongoing project has had it is ups and downs, year by year, but it is the fundamental reason the gorge is nowadays a well organised National Park run according to World Conservation Union standards.

The *agrimi* is a little mountain ibex, or wild goat, rather like a St. Kilda sheep, but with a black stripe down its back. An old

male with huge horns that would be valued by hunters may not exist in the wild at present. In the autumn, when food is scarce, 'tame' *agrimi* with their young forage for food behind

Starting down the gorge at Xyloscala

Samaria old village in spite of the many people gathered there at midday. They may also raid the litter bins by Ay. Nicolaos chapel (the first main stopping point on the route down) in the afternoon when most walkers have gone. Occasionally they leave the gorge. Amongst domestic goats nearby you may see half-breeds with black stripes down their backs.

A river fed by mountain springs and snow-melt runs down the gorge, disappearing and reappearing at intervals, which is typical of limestone terrain. Stepping stones are positioned at the many river crossings on the walk. For those who prefer to wade (bring sandals) the river is not fast-running by the time the gorge opens to the public on 1 May and its flow will lessen each week.

Principal man-made features are the old village of Samaria halfway down, from which the population was resettled in the 1960s, and the old village of Ay. Roumeli, just outside the park boundary at the bottom. New Ay. Roumeli is 1 kilometre further on, right on the sea shore. Other constructions in the gorge, apart from mule tracks, are chapels, ruined Turkish forts and water conduits to ruined sawmills or used for irrigation.

The park makes a significant cultural contribution by inducing town-dwelling Cretans to rediscover the beauty and worth of their own countryside and the pleasures of walking. Locals can choose their day: overcast, cool Sundays are preferred, when whole families can be seen trooping down alongside the tourists.

As this part of the south coast is free of roads, tour groups finish by being transferred from Ay. Roumeli to Hora Sfakion, or Souyia, by boat where they are met by the same coaches that took them up to Xyloscala. It is a long round for the bus drivers and an even longer day for the tourists. This standard tour method of hurrying down the gorge, and then leaving it almost immediately, detracts from the experience and does not fully reward the effort involved. Walk outside the 'rush hours' and make a point of staying overnight in Ay. Roumeli if you can.

Directions

The main trail is so well tramped that it is easy to follow and needs no signposting. Instead, signboards indicate points of interest. Wardens patrol the route throughout the day and a mule-borne rubbish-collection patrol operates late afternoon, after most walkers have gone. Keep your ticket; it is collected in as part of a census procedure at the other end.

Boat departures from Ay. Roumeli to Hora Sfakion are likely to be at 12.00, 15.45, 17.30 and 19.30 during the main tourist season. A skeleton service operates at other times. The 12.00 and the 15.45 boats usually call at Loutro. For Souyia, departure is likely to be at 16.00. Journey time in either direction is about 45 minutes, varying with the weather or a call at Loutro (an extra 30 minutes) or both. The last KTEL evening bus to Chania (usually packed) waits for the boat (see Public Transport section, page 14). The ticket kiosk with the latest timetables is at the bottom of Ay. Roumeli main street (see South Coast section, page 137). You can always enquire at the waterfront Tara restaurant (the landlord speaks English) if anything unusual seems to be happening.

The National Park entrance fee is about £3.00. It is open from 1 May to 31 October, depending on weather conditions. There are no commercial outlets inside the park. There is no camping.

A guide book is on sale at Xyloscala and Omalos. Drinking water, WCs and smokers' stopping places are provided at intervals. The Park closes at the top about 5 hours before the last boat leaves Ay. Roumeli (see South Coast section, page 137 and Walk 46).

Organised day tours have left Xyloscala by 14.00, so an early afternoon start allows you to walk down relatively undisturbed. Otherwise, start around 7.00am when the ticket kiosk opens, having stayed overnight on the plateau. Deliberately planning these alternative times is well worth it as this lovely walk is downgraded if too many people are doing it at the same time – a daily average of 2000 is normal. In spite of all this activity, the gorge is still a wild, rugged and potentially hazardous place. Always be on the alert for falling rocks – rain followed by wind dislodges them most readily. The park may be closed under these conditions. Tired or injured people, who finish the trip riding one of the few 'rescue' mules from Samaria village (which is expensive), sometimes hurt themselves further by falling off the mule, as the pack-saddles are extremely uncomfortable. On rare occasions desert-like flash floods occur, when the parched land cannot absorb the first storms of winter. It is sensible to be at least aware of this if a storm occurs. Unmaintained paths off the main trail are closed to the public (due to accidents in the past) and special permission from the Forestry Directorate of Chania is needed for access to them.

Towards the end of the walk, note the Turkish fort on the western skyline above the valley. The climb to it is not as far as it looks and for unhurried walkers (wearing boots) it makes an interesting and unconventional way of arriving at Ay. Roumeli (see Walk 47).

Walk 3. The Ascent of Gingilos

Grade:	C
Starting point:	Xyloscala (1,250m/4,100ft) – Omalos
Access:	KTEL Omalos bus or taxi from Chania
Finishing point:	Xyloscala
Access:	KTEL Omalos bus or taxi from Chania or walk to Omalos hamlet
Height of Gingilos:	2,080m (6,824ft)

Height gain:	from Xyloscala, 830m (2,723ft)
Approximate distance:	9km (5.5mls)
Time allowance:	Xyloscala to top of first spur (1,400m/4,593ft): 45mins; spur to Linoseli spring (1,500m/4,921ft): 45mins; spring to Gingilos saddle (1,800m/5,905ft): 1hr 10mins; saddle to summit: 50mins.
Ascent total:	3hrs 30mins
Descent:	summit to spur: 1hr 40mins: spur to Xyloscala: 30mins
Total :	5hrs 30mins
Variation:	spur direct to Omalos hamlet: 1hr 40mins.

The mountain with the huge grey crag opposite Xyloscala is called Gingilos. It is the most accessible high peak of the White Mountains. The ascent, on a well-beaten footpath, is a deservedly popular walk offering spectacular views from any level. As the return is down the same way, the walk can be curtailed at any stage. On part of the 45 minute final-ascent section, minor rock scrambling ability is needed, but hand and footholds are easy on the rough rock. As with all Lefka Ori peaks, high winds may affect the summit area and snow drifts may linger on steeper slopes in the early spring. Take no risks – alter your plans if conditions dictate. Take daysack essentials. For once you won't need to carry much water as Linoseli spring, which supplies Xyloscala, is halfway up the route to Gingilos.

At Xyloscala viewing terrace, on the west side, Gingilos crag is in front of you. Over to the south-east, Pachnes (2,453m/8,453ft), the highest peak of the Lefka Ori, rises beyond the east rim of the gorge. Up to the right, to the west, a massive scree slope is bordered by Gingilos crag. Note the patch of thorny burnet at its base, green in the spring and brown in the autumn, that marks the location of Linoseli spring. Note also the saddle on the skyline above the spring. The final pull to the summit is up to the point on the skyline to the left of this.

Directions

The footpath starts from the front steps of the restaurant above the viewing terrace and climbs the first hillside in easy-gradient zigzags. After 45 minutes, the spine of the low ridge above the Xyloscala road is reached. On the way down, if you want to head

Muletrack and cypress trees on the ascent of Gingilos (Walks 1 and 3)

for Omalos hamlet, take the goat paths down this spur and then cross the plateau on service tracks.

The footpath now crosses back towards the gorge and then turns in, heading for an area of rugged pinnacles beside the scree slope. Just before the path loses height to reach the pinnacles, note the goat paths (footpaths) ascending, right, to the top of the ridge.

For Koustoyerako: leave the path here for Strifomadi summit (Walk 6). *For Gingilos:* after passing through the pinnacles and a spectacular rock arch, the footpath gains height again for Linoseli, where there is a concrete tank and tin troughs in a clump of thorny burnet. The footpath continues from the spring, zigzagging up the firm side of the scree, alongside crags and boulders.

The saddle, a pleasant place to be on a settled fine day, thinly divides the Samaria and Tripiti gorges. Over to the east, the red-roofed Kallergi Refuge has been in view for some time with Melindaou behind, its great stratified cliff forming the north-east rim of the gorge. Lammageiers (bearded vultures) identifiable by their diamond-shaped tails, often soar above at midday. The largest birds in Europe, they roost on inaccessible crags of the

55

Tripiti Gorge. At any time elsewhere in the mountains these huge birds may be seen gliding by on a foraging trip.

Splintered paths continue up from the saddle to the south. On the first section, which is steep, when bare rock takes over from heathland, it's probably easier to climb up a little to the right of a pothole in the rocks. The route soon levels out before climbing again and rocks are variously waymarked: in general the route bears left. The tiny white chapel of Profitis Elias Tripitis is in view far below, to the west, on a crag where the Tripiti Gorge meets the sea near Souyia (Trek 10).

A large cairn marks Gingilos summit. A subsidiary rocky summit to the east lies nearer the rim of the gorge. Volakias (2,116m/6,942ft), the highest peak of the western massif, is next along the ridge to the south. To climb Volakias, first descend steeply from Gingilos summit to a small saddle that separates the two peaks. Return on a shepherds' route that contours from there, back to the Gingilos saddle. Beyond Volakias is a long crag-ridden, waterless ridge top between the Samaria and Klados gorges. From this ridge top there is a relentlessly steep 860m descent to Ay. Roumeli, the only way down – the whole venture is a Grade E expedition that needs a guide. To the west, across the Tripiti Gorge, part of Walk 6 to Koustoyerako is in view. Looking east, note the ridge leading up to Melindaou (Walk 5 and Trek 6) and then follow the profile of the mountains south from Pachnes to identify Zaranokefala and its summit crag (Trek 7).

Return down exactly the same way. Or, for Omalos instead of Xyloscala, peel off down the spur above the road. Keep more or less to the spine of this ridge right to its end, where you have a bird's eye view of the plateau's service tracks. Memorize this layout, because once you are level with the plateau you will not be able to see the track you want to use. Bear left now, for the final descent, and then follow the shepherds' footpaths that link to the main asphalted rim road and the service tracks.

Walk 4. Xyloscala to Kallergi Refuge

Grade:	A
Starting point:	Xyloscala (1,250m/4,100ft)
Access:	KTEL Omalos bus or taxi from Chania
Finishing point:	Kallergi Mountain Refuge
Access:	on foot from Xyloscala or via shepherds' road from the Omalos Plateau. A vehicle lift service is offered to and from Xyloscala, to order from Kallergi.
Height:	Kallergi Refuge: 1,680m (5,511ft)
Height gain:	430m (1,410ft)
Approximate distance:	3km (1.8mls)
Time allowance:	1hr 55mins.

Kallergi Refuge, perched high on the north-west rim of the gorge, was used for Greek Army training during the Greek military dictatorship (1967-74). Thereafter, the Chania EOZ took it over and leased it to mountain guide Joseph Schwemburger. As an upgraded mountain hut, Kallergi sometimes features in Greek Government courses designed to show Crete (and Greece) to young Greek nationals living abroad. Otherwise, from April to October, a steady flow of walking groups and freelance travellers sustains this busy alpine-style catering enterprise, Tel. (Chania) 0821 74560. Facilities include full board and bunkroom or roof space sleeping quarters. Rainwater collection from the roof does not stretch to inside showers and an eaves-hung water bag substitutes for this – filled from the additional water supply brought up from Chania. Bottled water and other drinks are expensive. This is a popular base for the ascents of Melindaou and Gingilos requiring a two or three-night stay and also a stopping point on the trekking route to Katsiveli and beyond. A shepherds' road (not for taxis) serves the refuge and then continues on under the northern flank of Melindaou.

Directions

Leave Xyloscala on the east side (where there is a water tap under a cypress tree) via the footpath signboard, which reads 1 hour 20 minutes to Kallergi. Within 40 minutes join the shepherds' road from the plateau and continue up on this – optional short cuts appear occasionally. A small stone-built shepherds' shelter with a Second World War memorial plaque marks the top. Kallergi is in sight, 5 minutes away. (Keep right – sometimes thick mist engulfs the cliff top.) Refreshments are available to passers-by.

Walk 5. Kallergi Refuge to Melindaou

Grade:	C
Start/Finish point:	Kallergi Refuge (1,650m/5,413ft) – a circular walk
Access:	Walk 4 from Xyloscala, or shepherds' road from Omalos Plateau
Height of Melendaou:	2,133m (6,998ft)
Height gain:	483m (1,583ft)
Approximate distance:	16km (10mls)
Time allowance:	Kallergi to Poria (1,500m/4,921ft): 50mins; Poria to top of ridge (1,840m/5,902ft): 1hr 10mins; ridge walk to Melendaou saddle (1,900m/6,233ft): 1 hr; saddle to summit: 1hr 15mins
Ascent total:	4hrs 15mins
Descent:	summit to Kallergi: 2hrs 30mins via E4 Trail
Total:	6hrs 45mins.

Using Kallergi Refuge (reservations Tel. 0821 74560) as a convenient starting point, Melindaou (2,133m/6,998ft) towering to the north-east above the Samaria Gorge, can be reached as a not too demanding day walk, allowing non-backpackers a chance of views in the heart of the range. As it is on the regular schedule of walking groups staying at Kallergi, the route is well tramped and partly waymarked. Kallergi is 50 minutes walk, on the shepherds' road, to the base of the long ridge leading up to Melindaou. For a circular walk, approach the peak from along the top of this ridge and then return to Kallergi by dropping down to the shepherds' road alongside it, on part of the E4 Trail.

Directions

From Kallergi walk east on the shepherds' road to Poria, an area of bracken-filled meadows at the foot of the long ridge. An old stone hut can be seen over on the right. Head straight for the steep hillside in front of you, south-east, and take splintered footpaths up to the ridge top.

Now overlooking the gorge and almost level with Melindaou's huge stratified cliff, start along one of the best ridge walks in Crete. This can take in one or two ridge top peaks. After about 50 minutes, arrive at a saddle below the steep ascent ridge to Melindaou summit. Note that the return route to Kallergi (E4 Trail poles) descends from this saddle, via a north-westerly traverse followed by a steep path down to the shepherds' road.

Just below the summit area, the E4 Trail, now safely above the stratified cliff, turns east for Potamos and Katsiveli (Trek 6). From the summit, where there is a trig point, Kaloros (1,925m/6,315ft), which dominates the mountains near Kolokithas, obscures the view down to Chania. (Note that a section of Trek 1 mule track is in sight.) The Potamos valley (Trek 5) shows 140 SE, with the Pachnes massif and Zaranokefala beyond it. Modaki (1,224m/4,016ft) one of several cone-shaped peaks of the Madares, rises above Katsiveli.

Walk 6. Xyloscala to Koustoyerako via Strifomadi

Grade:	D
Starting point:	Xyloscala (1,250m/4,101ft)
Access:	KTEL Omalos bus, or taxi from Chania
Finishing point:	Koustoyerako (500m/1,640ft)
Access:	taxi from Souyia
Height of Strifomadi:	1,942m (6,371ft)
Height gain:	692m (2,270ft)
Height loss:	1,442m (4,730ft)
Approximate distance:	14km (9mls)
Time allowance:	Xyloscala to goat path turn off (1,500m/5,712ft): 1hr; to Strifomadi summit: 1hr 50mins; summit to Achlada valley (1,600m/5,249ft): 1hr; Achlada to 1,000m (3,280ft) point: 1hr 50mins; to Koustoyerako 1hr 30mins. Total 7hrs 30mins.

This is a spectacular mountain route from the Omalos Plateau to Koustoyerako and Souyia. Branching off from the Gingilos footpath, it takes in Strifomadi summit before making a long descent to the south-west over hillsides high above the Tripiti Gorge. More centrally placed and just as accessible as Gingilos, Strifomadi offers a better all-round view, but the steep summit-approach makes this a walk rarely tackled by organised groups.

Descending in Spring with view of Omalos

This route suits from May–November, if the snowdrift under Strifomadi summit is passable. Take daysack essentials and a minimum of two litres of water. (For backpackers this walk makes a pleasant two-day route.)

Directions
Follow Walk 3 to the goat paths turn-off before the pinnacles. Ascend the ridge. A spindly iron fence borders the top edge of the cliff on the mountainside below Strifomadi summit. The footpath ascends near the fence until, after gaining most of the height, it traverses right to finish the climb on an easier gradient. If snowdrifts linger, the fence is a useful safety guide.

The summit is the highest point above the huge cliff at the head of the Tripiti Gorge. Beyond this gorge the route descends to the south-west down the bare hillside to trees at the foot of a watercourse (snow-melt). Further below, an isolated bare ridge runs east/west, above the high-level valley (1,500m/4,921ft) called Achlada. (Some maps mark it in the Tripiti Gorge, but Achlada is just north of an isolated pear-shaped ridge, almost in line with Koustoyerako.)

West from the summit, just clear of the cliff, turn quite steeply downhill, south. When the steep section ends, turn west, heading for the far side of the watercourse. On this section, as the path traverses the hillside, a tiny spring (bright green weed) emerges on the path. It may be dry by midsummer.

The watercourse is draining to a tributary ravine of the Tripiti Gorge. On reaching this, the path makes a short traverse above it, under cypress trees, to enter Achlada in a mass of thorny burnet where there is a cistern (poor water). The collapsed concrete roof of an old *mitato* ('mee-tat-toe') exposes its cheese store, which may suit as shelter in bad weather.

In 1943 this remote valley was the hideout of the Koustoyerako band of Second World War Resistance fighters led by New Zealander Dudley Perkins (see Books section, page 186).

Continue for 20 minutes down the valley on the footpath above the watercourse, to a concrete flat-topped cistern (good water) and a roofless stone hut. Check the water level in the goats' trough and replenish it if it is very low; it is a long mule ride up from Koustoyerako and someone has to come up to attend to this at intervals. Cross the river bed to rejoin the path as it enters the trees. Old charcoal-making sites in the oak forest and a *kalderimi* (paved mule track) that bypasses a drop of large boulders can be seen on the way down.

After about 3 kilometres (1.8 miles), at an altitude of 1000m (3.280ft), the river bed turns sharply left and south. Here mature pines survived the 1994 Souyia valley fire. Still very far below, the valley is glimpsed through the trees. Walk 7 from Ay. Theodoros comes in at this turning.

After about 12 minutes, with the river bed developing into a ravine, take a *kalderimi* ascending out of it, left. Follow this old trail over and down to a fenced concrete cistern and a road. Here the mountainside is cut to bits by roadworks and Koustoyerako is in sight, still quite far below, under the brow of Ochra crag.

Leaving the high level ravine below Achlada on the way to Koustoyerako

Village vineyards feature on a wide saddle beyond the pine forest. Descend via the road and sections of old footpath through woodland to this saddle with its large concrete village water tank (locked). Continue down the road. Leave the road at the first bend on a footpath under Ochra crag to the village. This unusually damp, north-facing crag sustains a mass of wild flowers in the spring.

Koustoyerako has two *kafeneia*, which may or may not be open. (If they can be found, village proprietors are pleased to open up if visitors arrive.) A Souyia taxi can be called. There are no rooms as Koustoyerako channels its enterprise into the beach resort of Souyia. However, trekking groups sometimes camp here (enquire).

It is possible to get down to Souyia on tracks and footpaths: allow 2 hours. Retrace your steps up to the *plateia* (main square) and bear right to leave the village on an unmade road contouring south under Ochra crag. Bear right off the road down to Livada village (seen below) and from there take a track down to the main river bed.

Walk 6a. Koustoyerako to Xyloscala via Strifomadi

Take a minimum of two litres of water.

This is Walk 6 in reverse.

Grade:	D
Starting point:	Koustoyerako (500m/1,640ft)
Finishing point:	Xyloscala (1,250m/4,101ft)
Height of Strifomadi:	1,942m (6,371ft)
Height gain:	1,442m (4,730ft)

Height loss:	692m (2,270ft)
Approximate distance:	14km (9mls)
Time allowance:	Koustoyerako to 1,000m (3,280ft) point: 2hrs 30mins; to Achlada cistern 1,300m (4,265ft):1hr 30mins; to summit: 3hrs; to Xyloscala: 2hrs. Total: 9hrs.

Directions

Leave the *plateia* at the top left-hand corner, on a short village lane to a footpath up through olive groves. Ascend under the north face of Ochra crag, and then turn up a road to a concrete water tank and vineyards. Aiming for the re-entrant in the mountainside now just above, east, bordered by a crag on the left, continue up, taking short cut footpaths across the loops. Bear left as the road divides. This road ends (1997) at a fenced concrete cistern. From here reverse Walk 6.

Walk 7. Omalos to Koustoyerako via Ay. Theodoros

Grade:	D
Starting point:	Omalos hamlet (1,050m/3,444ft)
Access:	KTEL Omalos bus or taxi from Chania
Finishing point:	Koustoyerako (500m/1,640ft)
Access:	taxi from Souyia
Height gain:	150m (492ft)
Height loss:	700m (2,296ft)
Approximate distance:	13km (8mls)
Time allowance:	Omalos hamlet to Ay. Theodoros chapel (1,100m/3,608ft): 50mins; chapel to last cistern (approx. 1,250m/4,101ft): 1hr; cistern to 1000m (3,280ft) point: 3hrs; to Koustoyerako: 1hr 30mins. Total: 6hrs 20mins.

Of the two traditional routes between Omalos and Koustoyerako this is the least strenuous, as it skirts the western flank of Psilafi, contouring at about 1,200m (3,937ft) high above the Ay. Irini Gorge and the Souyia valley. Traversing rough, waterless terrain, this is an unfrequented route offering wide open views across the valley. Take daysack essentials and a

63

minimum of two litres of water from the last cistern. Note the shepherds' roads extending from Ay. Theodoros and Koustoyerako are probably designed to link up in due course, and thus 'open up' this remote mountainside. This route will then become a long, but easy, road tramp.

Directions

Follow Walk 8 to Ay. Theodoros chapel on the western exit road. Just beyond the chapel, take the shepherds' road uphill, left. This quickly gains height to a 'shelf' high above the Souyia valley. Follow the road south to where it ends (1997) in a small hollow with a concrete water tank and cistern – the last water point on the route.

Red dots on the south side of the hollow direct you up a shallow gully to the top of the next hill. Beyond is a wide descending valley with various sheep paths. Make your way down (this is a rocky stretch) to about 1,200m (3,937ft) to get onto the best path for the continuing traverse. Your destination is the forested river bed descending from the Achlada valley (Walk 6). If you contour well above the crags of the Ay. Irini Gorge and keep within the tree line, you will eventually reach it even if you missed the best footpath.

As the river bed is approached, the forest thickens. The contouring route ends and a red-dotted path takes over, descending to 1000m (3,280ft) and the spot where the wide stony river bed, set in mature pines, makes a sharp turn from west to south. *For Koustoyerako:* follow Walk 6. *For Achlada:* turn east and walk up the river bed. When the trees end, cross the river bed to find the cistern on the northern bank.

Walk 7a. Koustoyerako to Omalos via Ay. Theodoros
Take a minimum of two litres of water.
This is Walk 7 in reverse.

Grade:	D
Starting point:	Koustoyerako
Finishing point:	Omalos hamlet
Height gain:	700m

Samaria old village in the heart of the gorge

Typical terrain of the northern slopes at high level, rugged rocks near Volikas refuge (Walk

Relaxing on the way to Spathi summit (Walk 12)

Height loss: 150m
Approximate distance: 13km (8mls)
Time allowance: 7hrs.

Directions

Leave the *plateia* at the top left-hand corner, on a short village lane to a footpath up through some olive groves. Ascend under the north face of Ochra crag, and then turn up a road to a concrete water tank and vineyards. Aiming for the re-entrant in the mountainside now just above, east, bordered by a crag on the left, continue up, taking short cut footpaths across the road loops. Bear left as the road divides. This road ends (1997) at a fenced concrete cistern. From here reverse Walk 7.

Walk 8. Omalos to Ay. Irini Gorge

Grade: B
Starting point: Omalos hamlet (1,050m/3,444ft)
Access: KTEL Omalos bus or taxi from Chania
Finishing point: Ay. Irini Gorge trailhead – north (600m/ 1,968ft)
Access: KTEL Souyia bus or taxi from Chania or Souyia
Height gain: 50m (164ft)
Height loss: 500m (1,640ft)
Approximate distance: 8km (5mls)
Time allowance: Omalos hamlet to Ay. Theodoros chapel: 50mins; to Ay. Irini gorge trailhead: 2hrs 10mins. Total: 3 hrs.

An asphalted road leaves from the western rim of the plateau passing the chapel of Ay. Theodoros. After contouring west for 8 kilometres it joins the main Chania to Souyia road at Seli, a narrow neck of land which is the only 'bridge' between the porous sedimentary rock of the White Mountains and the impervious metamorphic rock of the Selino region. Huge valleys descend north/south either side of this watershed. The Ay. Irini Gorge splits the southern valley as a deep gash just under the western flank of Psilafi. Opening out 5 kilometres from the shore, its river bed reaches the sea at Souyia, a beach resort.

Unlike the new road, the old mule track from Omalos to Ay. Irini takes a direct route down to the gorge to Souyia. However, road-surfacing work has tossed tons of scree over the *kalderimi* just where it zigzagged down the steepest slope. Shepherds (they would say 'roadworkers don't care about people') have been obliged to form a new footpath from the road to the mule track, but that new turn-off is 3 kilometres along the asphalt road from Ay. Theodoros chapel. Do not be too put off, for this is still an interesting and useful route out of the plateau even though the road relegates it to second-choice category. It is an easier route to Souyia than Walks 6 or 7.

Directions

Follow Walk 7 past Ay. Theodoros chapel and the shepherds' road. The old mule track runs west, parallel to the main road, and about 200m beyond the junction with the shepherds' road; red paint marks a place for joining it. (Alternatively, to avoid the scree crossing, continue on the road.)

After about 500m reach the scree crossing in amongst sparse trees. Here the *kalderimi* zigzagged downhill and so, with this part now buried, cross the scree and pick up the trail further down. (Take an escape path up to the road if you prefer and continue to the new footpath, which misses this whole section.) This steep hillside is just above a subsidiary ravine of the Ay. Irini Gorge. The Feigou robbers' path is routed down this ravine, but it is unfrequented and very steep and no easy short cut.

Beyond the scree, a fine stretch of *kalderimi* with a high retaining wall descends to a green spurge-covered valley. Cross to a flat concrete cistern, where there is good water, and then continue up in a north-westerly direction out of the valley. Another section of *kalderimi* clings to a crag, right, but as the limestone runs out, so does this paved track. Turn south down the spur on a footpath descending to a pine forest. Here another short section of well-built *kalderimi* leads down to a couple of houses, the river, and the bridge to the main Chania to Souyia road.

The Ay. Irini Gorge starts just on the left and is signed. It is also a KTEL bus stop: the 15.30 from Souyia to Chania passes about 16.00. Otherwise, walk north up the road to the first taverna (where there is a telephone) or continue down the gorge to Souyia: a walk of 4 hours.

Walk 9. Ay. Irini Gorge to Souyia

Grade:	B
Starting point:	On the Souyia road just north of Ay. Irini village (600m/1,968ft)
Access:	KTEL bus or taxi from Chania or Souyia (see details below)
Finishing point:	Souyia
Access:	KTEL Souyia bus or taxi (see details below)
Height loss:	600m (1,968ft)
Approximate distance:	8km (5mls)
Time allowance:	to Koustoyerako bridge: 3 hrs; to Souyia by road: 45mins; by river bed footpaths: 1 hr. Total: 4 hrs.

This short but varied gorge bordering the western flank of the White Mountains is a nature reserve of the Forest Directorate of Chania. Admission is free. WCs and water taps may not be operating early in the year. A river flows for some distance near the top, in spring, whilst at the bottom, patches of humidity and shade sustain a variety of plants. Gigantic ancient plane trees shade a flat clearing halfway down, and the trail is well tramped. This gorge is offered as a day tour excursion, but it is less visited than Imbros and Samaria because the Chania to Souyia road is narrow, long and winding, although it is a good scenic ride.

The walk starts from the main Chania to Souyia road just north of Ay. Irini village: a spot well known to taxi and bus drivers. From Chania: some taxi drivers may not want this job – just find another driver. From Souyia: taxi drivers are used to the road, but they are often busy so book in advance. (See the Public Transport section for bus service details, page 14)

Directions

Walk down to the refreshments kiosk and WCs in the woodland. From there the well-tramped, made-up footpath is easy to follow. Signboards mark the historic Feigou hideout where outlaws hid from the Turkish administration.

A car and bus park marks the end of the gorge. Continue along the road beside the river bed. For a more pleasant walk to the Koustoyerako bridge, turn off down an unsurfaced slip road to the right and cross the river bed to join the old track opposite. At the bridge turn right for the main road to Souyia. Otherwise make your way down the river bed on goat paths. The KTEL bus departs at 15.30.

For Lissos, an ancient, third-century BC site and spring, walk west to Souyia harbour where the E4 Trail waymarked footpath (to Paleochora) leads up a ravine. Allow 1 hour 15 minutes walking time to Lissos.

Walk 10. Omalos to Zourva

Grade:	D
Starting point:	Omalos hamlet
Access:	KTEL Omalos bus or taxi from Chania
Finishing point:	Zourva 600m (1,968ft)
Access:	Taxi from Chania or Fournes
Total height gain:	450m (1,476ft)
Total height loss:	800m (2,624ft): this is an undulating route
Approximate distance:	9km (5.5mls)
Time allowance:	Omalos hamlet to Forestry service cistern (800m/2,624ft): 1hr 5mins; cistern to Vothanou (1,000m/3,280ft): 1hr 15mins; Vothanou to Sterna (800m/2,624ft): 30mins; Sterna to inspection chamber (600m/1,968ft): 45mins; to ridge top (750m/2,460ft): 45mins; to Zourva: 50mins. Total 5hrs 10mins.

Losing height rapidly from the Omalos Plateau at first, this route then traverses three ridges of the northern foothills above Lakki. An unfrequented walk on shepherds' footpaths, it crosses only one road and has Amalia's taverna at Zourva as its destination.

Directions

From Omalos hamlet walk north on the main road to the plateau rim. (Note a last section of the old 'Mousourou Road' by a telegraph pole on the left.) Turn off right to a big concrete water tank. Clamber down on to a section of mule track running below and parallel to the road. In a few minutes this turns east as a footpath down a valley. Follow this footpath, passing areas of old terracing. The valley finally ends at a cypress-tree-filled cleft, which brings you out over a short, but steep, descent to a shepherds' road in a narrow valley. Turn left down this road for 200m to an old-style Forestry Service cistern.

For Lakki: continue down the road (Walk 11). *For Zourva:* leave the road at the cistern to ascend the next ridge east on a footpath. The footpath hardly shows, but knowing it is there, examine the ridge and note a dip in the skyline with a large rock and trees. The path climbs to this spot before gaining the top of the ridge from there.

Cross the river bed and bear right to find the path, which ascends steeply at first, before it turns left and heads towards a crag along an easy gradient. Ascend the crag and then continue up, with trees on your left. At the top, from which there are views, turn right up the spine of the ridge for a short distance to reach the main path traversing eastwards to the next descending spur. Climb over this spur and descend over old terracing to Vothanou, a high-level 'secret' valley (no cistern). Beyond it, to the east, a pipe conveying water to Meskla clings to the far side of a deep gorge.

Halfway along Vothanou, bear left through shady trees to the north rim. Make your way downhill, right, to mature oak trees on the descending spur, which is a place called 'Sterna' (*sterna* is the Greek word for cistern). Beside a big oak tree, a very old barrel-vaulted cistern (good water) is sited above the terracing that infills a small re-entrant. A broken concrete animal trough is imprinted (in Greek) with the name 'Kandidakis', a Lakkiot family, long since emigrated. Pass a ruined stone hut and shrine beyond the cistern and continue a short way down the ridge to where two bracken-filled gulleys descend steeply to the valley from the gorge. Pause here to note a shepherds' hut, almost directly opposite on the skyline of the next green ridge. A footpath leads down to Zourva from that hut.

Over old terracing, bracken and spurge, descend either gully to the valley below – and an (unlocked) inspection chamber of a water conduit. Needless to say, take care not to contaminate this village water supply.

Escape route to Lakki (of sorts): the footpath down the west side of this valley gains height around the end of the spur before descending through a very overgrown stretch to a confluence of gorges just below Lakki. From there it is 20 minutes up to the village (Walk 11). *For Zourva:* a path from the inspection chamber crosses the tree-lined river bed for the ascent of the next ridge. Climb to the hut and cistern (seepage well) on the ridge top. Zourva shows on the next ridge looking east and, just below, a shepherds' path heads for the village. After entering forest, it contours into a re-entrant before joining a vehicle track below Zourva. From behind a large sheep shed in the olive groves, a footpath leads left up to the main road: turn right for the taverna. Taxis can be called. Apart from her busy lunch hour trade, Amalia has twenty years experience of walkers' needs: a roaring stove on a wet day, an evening meal...

Walk 10a. Zourva to Omalos

This is Walk 10 in reverse.

Grade:	D
Starting point:	Zourva (600m/2,284ft)
Access:	Taxi from Chania
Finishing point:	Omalos hamlet (1,050m/3,444ft)
Access:	KTEL Omalos bus or taxi from Chania
Total height gain:	800m (2,624ft): this is an undulating route.
Total height loss:	400m (1,312ft)
Approximate distance:	9km (5.5mls)
Time allowance:	7hrs.

Directions

From the taverna, walk downhill past the War Memorial and then turn sharp left onto a gated footpath that descends to olive groves and a large shed. Take the track from the front of the shed for a minute or two, and then enter the forest by bearing left up a footpath. From there reverse Walk 10.

Walk 10b. Zourva to Meskla

Grade:	A
Height loss:	400m (1,312ft)
Approximate distance:	3km (1.8mls)
Time allowance:	50mins.

There are pleasant routes down to Meskla on the network of roads serving the olive groves of the valley on the eastern side of the Zourva ridge. The route described here is the shortest, but for a longer walk cross the valley to roads descending the far side.

Directions
Walk down the road from the taverna and take a footpath short cut from the chapel. Alternatively, follow the road, rounding the Zourva ridge until you overlook the next valley to the east. Just beyond the first inner U-bend descend right, on an unmade olive grove service road. After contouring round a re-entrant, keep left along under the Zourva ridge. Arrive at a Y-junction, where the left option heads uphill. Turn right and continue downhill, but thereafter keep left. Rejoin the main road. Leave it again on a steeply descending concreted lane on the left. On the village main road, the *kafeneon* is 300 metres past an old watermill, but it may be closed. The supermarket has a telephone (enquire at the house just above it). Meskla is on the KTEL weekday village schedule.

Walk 11. Omalos to Lakki and Meskla

Grade:	C
Starting point:	Omalos hamlet (1,050m/3,444ft)
Finishing point:	Lakki (500m/1,640ft)
Access:	KTEL Omalos bus or taxi from Chania
Height loss:	600m (1,968ft)
Approximate distance:	9km (5.5mls)
Time allowance:	Omalos hamlet to Stephanoporo hill (800m/2,624ft): 1hr 15mins; to below Lakki: 1hr 15mins; up to Lakki: 20mins. Total: 2hrs 50mins.

This is an old transhumance trail and a direct footpath between Lakki village and the grazing pastures of the Omalos Plateau. Lately it has become overgrown, but it is still a useful route for walkers.

Directions

Follow Walk 10 as far as the Forestry Service cistern, then continue down the shepherds' road to a sharp bend on the narrow saddle under the isolated spur.

This is the hill of Stephanoporo, where Second World War Special Operations Executive (SOE) agent Dudley Perkins and others were fatally ambushed in 1944.

Another old-style Forestry Service cistern is just below, at the head of a descending valley, whilst at the top of the shepherds' road, west, the Lakki–Omalos main road shows at a place called Fokyes. Fokyes is several kilometres by road from both Omalos and Lakki: these footpaths are much more direct.

Descend the valley filled with Jerusalem Sage, rounding the corner at the bottom, to head north-east towards a dry watercourse with cypress trees. Cross the watercourse to pick up an overgrown footpath descending beside the river bed, crossing it at intervals. The houses of Lakki come into view as the river bed turns north. The descent ends at a tree-filled confluence of ravines below the village. Ascend to the village past ancient olive trees.

Lakki has a small shop, *kafeneia*, tavernas and rooms and a church clock. It is on the KTEL bus route from Omalos to Chania.

For Meskla: walk north on the main road about 500 metres, around an outer bend, and then turn off right onto a service road that descends through olive groves.

Walk 11a. Lakki to Omalos

This is Walk 11 in reverse.

Grade:	C
Starting point:	Lakki (500m/1,640ft)
Finishing point:	Omalos hamlet (1,050m/3,444ft)
Access:	KTEL Omalos bus or taxi from Chania.

Height gain:	to plateau rim, 600m (1,968ft)
Approximate distance:	9 km (5.5mls)
Time allowance:	4hrs 25mins.

Directions

Leave Lakki via the concreted lane just under the terrace of Niko's Taverna and turn sharp left, downhill, just before a small concrete slaughterhouse. The overgrown footpath descends to a tree-filled confluence of ravines. Keep straight on up the ravine orientated north/south and from there follow the notes for Walk 11 in reverse.

THE NORTHERN FOOTHILLS

Introduction

The foothills of the White Mountains, in the districts of Kydonia and Apokorona, appear at first as a confusing mass of green spurge-covered ridges, spurs, valleys, gorges and ravines. Rainfall is much higher here than on the south coast. In Spring, areas of lush vegetation contrast with the snow-capped mountains above. Here are old terraces carpeted with wild flowers, steep hillsides of shrubs in colourful bloom and pockets of surprisingly varied woodland. At the tree line, dark green cypresses adorn rocky hillsides, and higher still steep bare mountainsides form some of the roughest and least-visited terrain of the entire range.

The old trails of Apokorona, with their good water supply and easily-cut sandstone, are dotted with the modest ruins and relics of a sensitive pastoral culture still remembered. Vineyards and olive groves concern villagers here, rather than tourism, and sheep raising is still important: shepherds of the foothills are well known to their counterparts across the mountains in Sfakia ('we are colleagues, you see').

Footpaths featured here, which would have been in much better condition decades ago, are among those that were used by George Psycoundakis on his journeys between Askyfou and Omalos. (George Psycoundakis is 'The Cretan Runner' in the book of the same name – see Books, page 186 – a member of the Second World War Resistance.) Sections of the 'northern traverse', just under steeper mountain slopes (Walks 13,14,16,18) were on the German Mountain Brigade's projected quick dash to Krappis to cut off the Allied retreat – an operation foiled by Greek rearguard defenders of the Alikanos valley.

Ongoing depopulation has rendered many old trails overgrown and it may be some time before these footpaths are reclaimed for recreational walking. Scratchy plants are never pleasant, but with long clothing, and the patience to ease through slowly, many routes are still negotiable. Cut out a thorn branch or two along the way if you have time. The villages of the foothills are on the KTEL village schedule (see Public Transport).

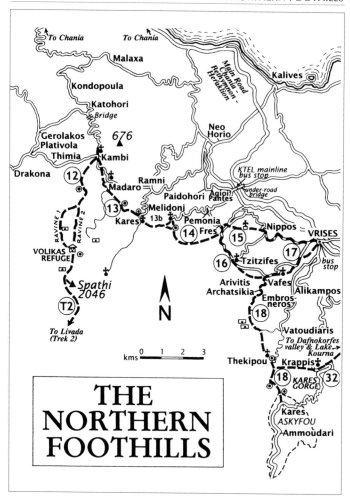

To Chania   To Chania

Malaxa

Kondopoula

Katohori
Bridge

Kalives

Neo
Horio

Main Road
Chania -
Rethymnon -
Heraklion

Gerolakos
Plativola
Thimia   Kambi   676 ▲

Drakona

KTEL mainline
bus stop

under-road
bridge

12

RAVINE 1
RAVINE 2

Madaro   Ramni

Paidohori Agioi
Pantes

13

Melidoni
Kares   13b   Pemonia
Fres

14

15

Nippos

VRISES

17

bus
stop

VOLIKAS
REFUGE

16   Tzitzifes

Arivitis   Vafes
Archatsikia   Alikampos

Embros-
neros

18

▲ Spathi
2046

T2

N

Vatoudiaris
*To Dafnokorfes
valley & Lake
Kourna*

To Livada
(Trek 2)

kms 0 1 2 3

Thekipou   Krappis

18   32

KARES
GORGE

THE
NORTHERN
FOOTHILLS

Kares
ASKYFOU
Ammoudari

Kambi

Attractively sited on a fertile shelf above a large cultivated upland valley, inland from Chania, Kambi at 600m (1,968ft) is the highest village of the foothills. For trekkers, one of the traditional north/south routes over the mountains, via the Volikas EOZ Refuge, starts here. A continuous low-level traverse all the way to Askyfou also starts here (unless you do not mind long road-tramps, in which case you could begin at Zourva or Drakona).

In a nearby outlying hamlet, a *kafeneon* run by Harethimo Nicoliodakis (ask for 'Ha-ree-thee-mo') is also a small shop. This is a quiet place, far from the tourist trail. The stock includes a few gas cylinders, some tinned foods, rice and pasta and there may be *graveira* cheese and eggs – and bread if deliveries permit. It may also be possible to arrange a self-catering overnight stay, as there are rooms and beds to spare.

The most noticeable feature beside the shop is the plane tree mentioned by Capt. Spratt RN, a topographical surveyor, who undertook an ascent of Ay. Pnevma (2,254m/7,394ft) from Kares in 1860. Note the way it has been pollarded, perhaps to make it fit the *plateia* of an earlier age. Capt. Spratt stopped here because the old road to Kambi, a *kalderimi* now engulfed by abortive terrace-forming and thorn thickets, climbed the hillside just below this point. Ruined houses throughout the valley bear witness to the Nazi occupation from 1941-44.

Walk 12. Kambi to Volikas Refuge (E4 Trail)

Grade:	C
Start/Finish point:	Kambi (600m/1,968ft) – a circular walk
Access:	KTEL Kambi bus or taxi from Chania
Height gain:	880m (2,887ft)
Height loss:	880m (2,887ft) (circuit)
Approximate distance:	14km (9mls)
Time allowance for	
Ascent:	Kambi to Volikas Refuge (1,480m/4,855ft): 3hrs 30mins
Descent:	via Volikas ravine: 2 hrs; via west ravine: 2hrs 45mins
Total for circuit:	5hrs 30mins, or 6hrs 15mins.

Volikas Refuge

This mountain walk to the limit of the tree line, with Volikas Refuge as its objective, is a particular delight in the spring when wild pear trees are in blossom and the snow has recently melted in the high meadows. Volikas is one of several mountain refuges in Greece dating from the 1950s when all materials had to be brought up by mule. Solidly built, with steel doors and shutters, these buildings have weathered decades of winter storms. Contact the EOZ in Chania to arrange an overnight stay. Otherwise, passers-by can use the spring and a utility shed alongside is left unlocked. A Madaro to Kambi shepherds' road is due to 'open up' this mountainside, but it does not yet reach the spring and refuge (1998).

This walk is suitable at any time of year if conditions are settled, and the snowline is above 1,500 metres (4,921 feet).

Face the panoramic view of the northern Lefka Ori, ideally from Capt. Spratt's plane tree, which overlooks the valley. Note two forested ravines over the low hills above Kambi. Volikas can be seen (through binoculars) just above the tree line at the top of the second ravine, to the east. The highest peak on the skyline is Spathi (2,046m/6,712ft), a 4.5 hour round trip from the refuge (Trek 2), and left of it is Ay. Pnevma, its long approach-ridge accessed from Kares or Melidoni. This walk to

the refuge ascends the second ravine. An option is to descend the first ravine, to the west, for a circular walk.

Directions

From Kambi *plateia*, pass in front of the church on the asphalt road heading straight for the mountains. After 5 minutes, bear right at a junction (signed for Plativoli). Turn left at the next junction, onto a track skirting a vineyard, and continue south to a sheep shed. Here turn up left on a waymarked footpath and go right passing through a gate to get onto the hillside. Splintered paths climb to a shepherds' road immediately above. Follow this, heading south-east, across the low hills to the gully formed by the first ravine.

Just across the gully, leave the road on splintered footpaths that climb the hillside. Various footpaths then head for the Volikas ravine providing a number of options – the best is waymarked with a few red dots, and there are cairns. In the ravine, cypress trees shade the old trail, which is built up in places. When it opens out, continue straight on up through the next cleft. As this opens out, the refuge is in sight on the hill above, due south. The footpath climbs this last stretch by first traversing to the left.

From the refuge terrace, face the crag. About 400m to the left, note a patch of green creeper in the crag. This marks the spring – a small but steady drip from the rock face collected into a large concrete cistern. Cross the hillside below a line of rocks to get to it.

Either retrace your steps for the easiest return to Kambi or head for the neighbouring ravine, which makes a more interesting round trip. Take the footpath traversing west from the refuge into a small rocky gully. Climb the west rim of this to get onto a descending footpath. After about 200m, note a large complex of old *mitatos*, like a pile of rocks, on the hillside below to the north-west.

Bearing left, descend a shallow gully orientated north/south, and then head for the *mitatos*. Behind you under the hillside is another old stone hut, once used by Kambi villagers to hide Second World War Allied army escapees after the Battle of Crete. The Volikas spring is the nearest functioning water supply. Just beyond the *mitatos* descend a steep gully to a flat-floored valley.

On the west side of this, enter trees and bear left over a large rock to pick up the path that descends to the top of the first ravine. The footpath down the ravine crosses from side to side, but finishes up on the west side. Emerging above the low hills, descend almost straight down to the shepherds' road. Turn left and west to retrace your steps to Kambi.

Walk 13. Kambi to Melidoni

Grade:	B/C
Starting point:	Kambi (600m)
Access:	KTEL Kambi bus or taxi from Chania
Finishing point:	Melidoni (400m)
Access:	Taxi from Vrises
Height loss.	This is an undulating route with a basic height loss of 200m (656ft)
Approximate distance:	10km (6mls)
Time allowance:	Kambi to Kares: 2hrs 40mins; Kares to Melidoni: 1hrs 20mins: Total 4hrs.

Far from the tourist trail, this walk links four hill villages: Kambi, Madaro, Kares and Melidoni. Apart from a few short sections on roads, the route is on shepherds' footpaths over a series of low ridges in an almost forgotten pocket of rural Apokorona.

Directions
From Kambi *plateia*, pass in front of the church on the asphalt road heading south straight for the mountains. After 5 minutes bear left at a junction that is signed to Madaro ('Mathe-ar-RO'). After 5 minutes leave the road to the left on a track to some sheep sheds: 2 minutes. Here bear right on to a section of the old road to Madaro, a pleasant short cut across this small valley. Rejoin the asphalt road and walk uphill as far as an old stone house with a green door. The road now loops around an open valley, but the olive grove provides a short cut: turn down to the right, keeping left on the track, and arrive at a clearing: 2 minutes. Turn sharp left and after 2 minutes, turn right on to a cobbled mule track. This ends at an old shrine and rejoins the asphalt road just

opposite a road to Ramni. Turn right, heading south, for the now unavoidable 10 minute walk on the main road to Madaro.

Shepherds live here and dogs will bark noisily at your arrival. The road ends at a turning circle, as Madaro's cluster of houses is on the end of a spur. The summit ridge of Mt. Ida is in view, far to the east.

Turn down right on a concrete-surfaced track (the shepherds' road to high pastures) passing the village church (water tap). Just beyond the church leave the road alongside a stone wall on an overgrown footpath which leads down to a dry river bed. From the opposite bank a section of paved *kalderimi* ascends a forested knoll to join the shepherds' road, which has skirted the valley. Old terracing and abandoned meadows here, partly engulfed by the woodland, might yield interesting flowers in the spring.

Follow the road up to the crest of the ridge. Turn off it 100m further on, down a footpath alongside a fence. (The road continues up the mountainside to its destination near Volikas.) Follow this path heading east up to the next ridge top, the first of four ridges on the way to Kares. Cross the spindly fence at the top and although your next objective is the re-entrant below, to the right, first follow the path left for about 100m to a pile of stones, which are part of a ruined boundary wall. (The path continues up to a huge oak tree near the ridge top where, intriguingly, there are old seepage wells.) Turn downhill from the pile of stones to pick up another path just below and head back straight for the re-entrant.

On the ascent of the next ridge, pass a tree with a flat rock set in its lower branches: a nice shady seat for one person. The next ridge after that is much higher, but the (splintered) path maintains an easy gradient on the climb. An old round stone shepherds' shelter lies just beyond the crest: from there, continue down into the next re-entrant. Just over the top of the next lower ridge, another huge deciduous oak has a fig tree growing in a fork. Across the valley a large stone-walled, tree-filled enclosure is the next objective – pass alongside its top wall. In 1992 a devastating bush fire raged through this region, but the trees inside the enclosure escaped.

Follow the *kalderimi* down to a gate made out of a wooden pallet and ascend to an abandoned roadwork. Cross a shepherds' road (heading up to a deep valley under Spathi) to pick up the mule track again for the short descent to Kares *plateia*.

Road access to Kares is long and involved, so that Kares *plateia* with its huge plane trees and ancient water source is definitely 'sleepy'. On the far side, opposite the spring, a small *kafeneon* opens in the late afternoon to suit the locals: passers-by are welcome to picnic here if it is closed. No food is on sale, as there is no demand for it. Locals say they get everything they need down in Neo Horio. Kares' vineyards are on the next ridge looking east, and this is also the way to Melidoni.

From the War Memorial to local patriots 'fallen heroically in battle', including, as ever, so many in early twentieth-century Balkan conflicts, cross the dry river bed on the road up to the church, which has a large canopy. Keep straight on up a *kalderimi* that ends beside a house on an ascending service road. Turn right, to bear left at the next junction. At the end of this straight section ascending the ridge heading north and arrive at a steel-tube gate. Climb above the road to rejoin the mule track; follow it for 1 minute to the crest of the ridge, where there is a Y-junction of paths – turn left.

A deep ravine lies between the Kares and Melidoni ridges, now in view to the east. Pause here to examine the profile of Melidoni ridge for an advance understanding of the next stage. Over on the far left, to the north-east, a lone vertical cypress tree punctuates the skyline. Note the high-level hillside terracing in front of it. On a gradual ascent from the ravine bed just below, the footpath heads for this feature. It is not as far as it looks.

Keep north on the walled mule track that descends to the ravine bed. Apokorona shepherds may block old paths with piles of branches. This directs sheep here and there; it is not intended to stop people from walking through – very few pass as it is. Clamber over the branches.

The waymarked trail now makes a long, straight traverse and then ascends over old terracing to a thin, rocky, descending spur, where an olive tree grows mixed in with a prickly oak. This spot is quite high above the ravine. Note a large weather-eroded outcrop of grey rock just across the re-entrant. The footpath passes above this. Turn up sharp right and then head straight across old terracing, choked with Jerusalem Sage, to a shady shelf

81

in the re-entrant. The Akrotiri Peninsular is in view far to the north-west. Beyond the big rock the footpath bears right, up to a crag in sparse trees, on this last part of the ascent to the hillside terracing. Cross to the low crag on the far side of the terracing. Climb up through it and bear right to pick up the footpath down the ridge. This meets an olive grove service road. Continue down to a road junction. Turn left, to head north-west, and, keeping straight on past a big cypress tree, walk down to a large fenced flat concrete cistern. Turn right for Melidoni, down the village street bordered with terrace-retaining walls.

Melidoni has two *kafeneia*. At Nico's, with its nice old-fashioned name 'The Will' (translation) the landlady can rustle up a hot meal. On sale are items a trekker might need such as gas cylinders and tinned food. Taxis can be called from here (enquire).

Walk 13a: Melidoni to Kambi

This is Walk 13 in reverse.

Grade:	B/C
Starting point:	Melidoni (400m/1,312ft)
Access:	Taxi from Vrises
Finishing point:	Kambi (600m/1,968ft)
Access:	KTEL Kambi bus or taxi from Chania
Height gain.	This is an undulating route with a basic height gain of 200m (656ft)
Approximate distance:	10km (6mls)
Time allowance:	Melidoni to Kares: 1hr 20mins; Kares to Kambi: 2hrs 40mins. Total: 4hrs.

Directions

Leave Melidoni *plateia* heading south, up the road with the terrace-retaining walls. At the T-junction, turn left and east. In 10 minutes, the Y-junction with a big cypress tree is reached. Keep right, and then turn up right at the next junction. The route is red-dot waymarked.

Walk 13b: Melidoni – Kares vineyards – Melidoni

Grade:	B/C
Start/Finish point:	Melidoni – a circular walk
Access:	Taxi from Vrises
Height gain/loss:	This is an undulating route between levels of 100m (328ft). Height gain/loss is about equal.
Approximate distance:	7.5km (4.6mls)
Time allowance:	3hrs.

From Melidoni, footpaths of the two ridges featured in Walk 13 make a round walk.

Directions

Follow Walk 13a to the steel-tube gate at the top of the Kares ridge. Pass through the gate and follow the vineyard service road along the ridge through two gates and down to a rocky outcrop, from which there are good views. To the right of it, an overgrown footpath leads straight downhill to the road below Melidoni, via a patch of burnt-out forest.

Walk 14. Melidoni to Fres

Grade:	B/C
Starting point:	Melidoni (400m/1,312ft)
Access:	Taxi from Vrises
Finishing point:	Fres (200m/656ft)
Access:	Taxi from Vrises
Height loss:	200m (656ft)
Approximate distance:	5km (3mls)
Time allowance:	1hr 40mins.

Melidoni has vineyards and olive groves, but it is also a shepherding village with a road to high pastures under Ay. Pnevma (2,254m/7,395ft), the next mountain east of Spathi. This walk follows the shepherds' road at first, but then peels off down the fairly rugged footpaths of the Fres ravine. As foothills' scenery goes, this is not the prettiest of walks, but as

Descending to Kambi (Walk 12)

part of a long distance traverse to Askyfou it is a pleasant way of avoiding the main road – or it extends the day walk from Kambi.

Directions

From Melidoni *plateia*, retrace your steps to the big cypress tree. Melidoni's mature pine forest was destroyed by a fire in 1992, but this tree survived the inferno. Two ancient seepage wells blend in so well just beside it that you could easily miss them. Keep to the left and continue east to a low pass on the next ridge, 1.5 kilometres from Melidoni.

In view from this pass is a large, open valley at the foot of the ravine descending from hillsides under Ay. Pnevma. Outcrops of unsightly black 'cinders' rock occur in places. On the far side, beyond the olive groves, a spurge covered ridge borders the side of the ravine. The route to Fres is down the ravine's dry river bed.

Leave the pass downhill, going east, and follow the road as it loops right around the olive grove and back towards the river bed. (Short cuts are fenced off.) Leave the road on any suitable path down to the river bed. A large concrete water storage tank is on the opposite bank, further up the valley. Various sheep paths descend the river bed. As it develops into a gorge, bear left, above the west bank. Stay on this path until, as the gorge ends, it descends steeply to a road-head by a chapel on top of a free-standing rock. Take the road and pass through an ugly gate. (Raise this whole contraption up to open it.) Bear left for Fres *plateia*, entered through an arched passage.

Fres has several *kafeneia* and shops. Taxis can be called from Vrises (enquire).

Walk 15. Fres to Vrises

Grade:	A
Approximate distance:	5km (3mls)
Time allowance:	1hrs 15mins.

A 2 kilometres short cut between Fres and Nippos improves this walk, which is otherwise on the main road.

Directions
From the church in Fres *plateia*, walk northwards down the street to a crossroads with a many-looped shrine. Turn right, heading east, and keep straight on past the cemetery. About level with an old restored monastery turn right downhill to the river bed below. This section may be overgrown or blocked with branches. Cross the leafy river bed to join an asphalt road looping to the right around a small valley. Beside an old burnt-out bus, turn up a village lane to join the main road from Fres to Vrises, where you turn left, passing the War Memorial. Vrises is now 3 kilometres on the asphalt road – turn left, north, at the next T-junction. Arriving in Vrises' main street, turn right for the KTEL bus station, shops and restaurants.

Vrises is a busy place which has attracted residents from the foothills' villages. KTEL buses for Chania, Rethymnon, Heraklion, and Sfakia, stop here.

Walk 16. Fres to Vafes via Tzitzifes

Grade:	A
Starting point:	Fres plateia (200m/656ft)
Finishing point:	Vafes (250m/656ft)
Access:	Taxi from Vrises
Height gain:	50m (164ft)
Approximate distance:	5km (3mls)
Time allowance:	1hr 30mins.

After 2 kilometres on the main road this follows a section of the old mule track to Vafes ('Va-FESS').

Directions
Leave Fres *plateia* on the main road heading south-east to Tzitzifes, 2 kilometres distant. Enter the village and pass first one cheese-making dairy and then another – in what appears to be a block of flats. Almost opposite, take an unmade road uphill towards the rear of the village church on the wooded hill beyond. At a Y-junction level with the cemetery, bear left keeping straight on to a first bend. This overlooks a section of old mule track now seen disappearing into the undergrowth in the direction of Vafes. Clamber down on to this old trail, which soon loses height over a big flat rock. Pass though a gate. A very fine stretch of old road now follows, but it is hopelessly overgrown with trees that are at least thirty years old. Alternative paths negotiate impassable places and by this means descend to the olive grove in the next valley. Here the old road, now almost entirely engulfed by undergrowth, makes a sharp left turn. Below this, and parallel to it, a footpath runs north to rejoin the road from the church. Turn right, uphill, to reach a junction with an asphalt road. Bear right for a hamlet that is, in effect, Upper Vafes. The old road following the lie of the land passed through here, although most traces of it have lately been replaced with concrete. Vafes main village is now below, its old houses clustered on an isolated hill. Several are restored as holiday homes. Descending from Upper Vafes, pass to the left, and below, the old school house in its grove of shady pines where there are seats, WCs and a water tap.

The main village has two *kafeneia* and a small shop selling some basics, including bread.

Walk 17. Vafes to Vrises

Grade:	A
Starting point:	Vafes (250m/820ft)
Access:	Taxi from Vrises
Finishing point:	Vrises (100m/328ft)
Height loss:	150m (492ft)
Approximate distance:	4km (2.5mls)
Time allowance:	1hr 10mins.

This walk uses the old mule track as a downhill short cut.

Directions

Walk downhill on the Vafes main road, then bear right heading for the church and cemetery. Just beyond the church a massive new circular water storage cistern and associated works supplies the fast-expanding village of Vrises. The old mule track from Vafes to Vrises descends alongside the north-east wall of the cemetery and joins the main road at the foot of the hill.

Turn right on the main road and follow this heading north to a bridge over the river-bed, east. Cross this for a back road route to Vrises that emerges at the main street beside the War Memorial. Turn left across the bridge for the bus station.

Walk 17a. Vrises to Vafes

This is Walk 17 in reverse.

Grade:	A
Height gain:	150m (492ft)
Approximate distance:	4km (2.5mls)
Time allowance:	1hr 30mins.

Directions

Leave Vrises behind the War Memorial and walk south past orchards and olive groves. Near a small waterworks station, bear right. Cross a bridge and turn left on to the main road to Vafes. As the road rounds the steep wooded hill in front of you, look out for the start of the old mule track on the left. Keep left as this climbs the hill to Vafes church. The village is about 1 kilometre uphill from the church.

Walk 18. Vafes to Askyfou

Grade:	C
Starting point:	Vafes (250m/820ft)
Access:	Taxi from Vrises
Finishing point:	Askyfou, Ammoudari (790m/2,591ft)
Access:	KTEL Sfakia bus or taxi from Chania or Vrises
Height gain:	to plateau rim, 650m (2,132ft)
Height loss:	110m (360ft)
Approximate distance:	10km (6mls)
Time allowance:	Vafes to Achatsikia (400m/1,312ft): 50mins; Achatsikia to TheKipou (800m/2,624ft): 2hrs 30mins; to plateau rim (650m/2,132ft): 1hr 20mins; to Ammoudari: 1hr. Total: 5hrs 40mins.

In his introduction to George Psycoundakis' Second World War memoirs *The Cretan Runner*, Patrick Leigh Fermor describes their first meeting 'in a thicket above Vafes'. Looking up at the steep shrub and spurge-covered crags above the village, you might wonder where this hide out could have been. However, above the crags rather different territory unfolds. The road zigzagging uphill immediately across from the *kafeneia* serves two old shepherding hamlets much further up the mountainside. In the days of mule transport these were convenient routes to the high pastures and many shepherds, with their knowledge of the mountains, were inevitably involved in Resistance activities.

From the Vrises to Sfakia KTEL bus, as it approaches Krappis, you may have seen, looking to the west across forested ridges, the little white chapel of Ay. Pnevma, on top of an isolated hill. The shepherds' footpath to Askyfou has to keep above a series of ravines, and in doing so, it passes behind this chapel before ascending the rim of the Askyfou Plateau.

Directions

Join the road to the high-level hamlet (called a *metochi* in Greek) of Archatsikia ('Ar-shat-seek-ya'), by bearing left at the next road junction beyond the *kafeneia*. The hillside levels out above the crags and here a woodland of deciduous oaks comes as a pleasant surprise, as it cannot be seen from the village. As the woodland ends, open views to the east include a little white chapel, called Profitis Ilias, on top of a steep spur. Road access to this chapel, although not in sight, is from Embrosneros. Continue up the road to Archatsikia, which has six inhabitants. ('We had twenty children here once, but all of them have emigrated.')

Continue up the road to a sharp U-bend. Here the road heads west for the next hamlet called Arivitis, which is uninhabited. In itself Arivitis might make a focal point for a walk above Vafes, although its old footpath, Vafes direct, is probably overgrown.

Leaving the road at the U-bend, keep straight on south on a footpath contouring around the hillside to a fenced enclosure. Make your way to the top of the enclosure to enter a high-level 'hidden' valley, served by a road from Vatoudiaris. Looking uphill to the south-east across the valley towards the Askyfou Plateau, note a forested ascending gully – the path to Ay. Pnevma chapel and TheKipou ('Theh-KEEpou') is routed up this.

Now take the valley road heading east as it loses height to round a spur above a steep ravine. This thin spur is almost entirely demolished by the bulldozed road. Gain height again, past sheep sheds, and keep straight on beyond the crest of the hill on a footpath heading for the forested gully. The road itself descends to Vatoudiaris, probably after many kilometres, but it would serve as an escape route. (There are several old, overgrown footpaths up and down these spurs and ridges, but exploring them requires a lot of time.)

Ascend the forested gully to a small open valley with old terraces. Three routes lead out of this valley: traverse left around a crag, for an uphill route that has no shade, or ascend left up a gully, or right, up another gully. Take the second option – it leads through a cypress tree-filled cleft, to eventually reach a small flat-floored hollow. Leave this via its east rim on a sheep track, and descend to the newly cut road just below. This is the road to Ay. Pnevma chapel (no water), left, on the hilltop to the north-east. Turn right for TheKipou, a clearing in the forest where there is a cistern with passable water, but no shelter. Leave TheKipou on the shepherds' road heading east. Beyond the trees, Krappis and the Vrises to Askyfou main road is in sight on the far side of the valley and Askyfou's steep plateau rim is directly above.

For Krappis: (taverna and bus stop) walk down the road to a flat area with a sheep-shed from where footpaths lead east to Krappis. *For Askyfou:* climb the steep but shallow gully now on your right to reach the first valley of the plateau rim. Here there is a cistern (good water) and a shady grove of prickly oaks. At the far end of the valley, a footpath ascends to join the shepherds' road to Niato (Walk 27). This would suit as an escape route in bad weather, although it is a long tramp down to Askyfou. Instead, on entering the rim valley, bear left up its east side on a path to another valley, from where a distinct shepherds' trail descends south to the Askyfou main road. A new road, replacing this mule track, is under construction (1998). Turn right for Ammoudari.

THE ASKYFOU PLATEAU

Introduction

The Askyfou Plain (called 'Plateau'), at 700m, is lower than the Omalos Plateau. Its location on the main road to the south coast makes it habitable all the year round, even though it may be snowed in for some days in winter. Askyfou's most distinguishing feature is a Turkish fort sited on the highest knoll. The fort is one of several built after the failed 1866 Revolution during the struggle for independence.

This is a Sfakiot mountain community and the main agricultural occupation is shepherding. Two cheese dairies, which operate from April to June, supply outlets in Chania. Seepage wells on the valley floor allow the cultivation of cereals, potatoes and vines: crops that reflect the changing seasons in a patchwork of meadows. In Spring carpets of wild flowers add blazes of colour.

Three of the four villages of the plateau stretch out along the road skirting the western side. The main village is Ammoudari. Its roadside *plateia* (overlooked by a whitebeam tree and monuments to local heroes) is also the main bus stop. The bus crew call this bus stop Askyfou ('As-KEE-foo'). There are rooms, tavernas and *kafeneia* in Ammoudari. A few minutes from the *plateia,* along the road to the south, is the village of Petres where there is a supermarket stocking everything a trekker needs. It is open from 8am until 10pm daily. There are bakeries at Ammoudari and Kares – and *kafeneia* in every village except Goni ('Gon-NEE').

At Kares a collection of weaponry, equipment and bric-a-brac, jettisoned by Allied forces retreating after the 1941 Battle of Crete, awaits proper housing. Ask for the m*useo*. Interested visitors may be plied with *raki* as they discuss this historic event well within living memory.

Just a few traces of the old road still survive to reveal that Goni, now very isolated across the plateau on a rocky knoll, was once right on this road. Following the lie of the land over the pass behind the fort, the old road continued south to Imbros along the eastern edge of the plateau.

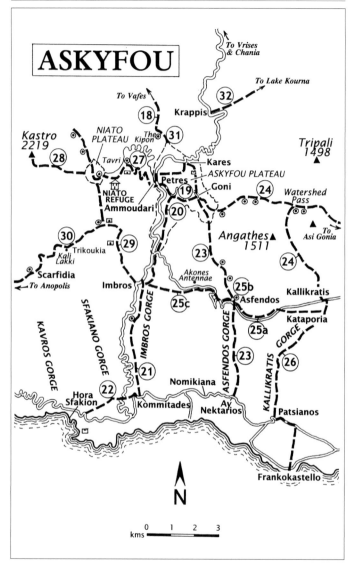

ASKYFOU

To Vrises & Chania

To Lake Kourna

To Vafes

Krappis ③②

⑱

③①

Kastro 2219

NIATO PLATEAU

The Kipon

Tripali 1498 ▲

㉘

Tavri

㉗

Kares

ASKYFOU PLATEAU

NIATO REFUGE

Petres

Goni

Ammoudari

⑲

㉔

Watershed Pass

⑳

To Asi Gonia ▲

㉚

㉙

Angathes ▲ 1511

㉓

㉔

Trikoukia

Kali Lakki

Scarfidia

To Anopolis

Imbros

Akones Antennae

㉕c

㉕b

Asfendos

Kallikratis

㉕a

Kataporia

KAVROS GORGE

SFAKIANO GORGE

IMBROS GORGE

ASFENDOS GORGE

KALLIKRATIS GORGE

㉑

㉖

㉒

Nomikiana

㉓

Hora Sfakion

Kommitades

Ay Nektarios

Patsianos

N

Frankokastello

0 1 2 3
kms

Several good walks extend from Askyfou although only a few of them are circular. The KTEL Chania to Sfakia schedule helps with this problem.

To the west, Kastro (2,218m/8,446ft) rises beyond the plateau rim. After the Gingilos group and Melindaou, this is the most accessible peak of the range. From the Niato Plateau at the foot of Kastro, paths lead south to Anopolis, or Imbros, and E4 Trail poles mark one end of a challenging east/west mountain traverse via Kastro's north flank.

Just behind Goni a distinct divide in the mountainous rim marks the old mule track to Asi Gonia. Asfendos and Kallikratis can also be reached from Goni. The old road can still be followed as a walkers' short cut to Hora Sfakion via the Imbros Gorge. There is also Walk 18 in reverse, to Vafes, and lastly, by taking the bus to Krappis, you could follow Askyfou's old transhumance trail down to Lake Kourna and Georgioupoli.

Walk 19. Around the Plateau

Grade:	A
Start/Finish point:	A circular walk from Ammoudari
Access:	KTEL Sfakia bus or taxi from Hora Sfakion or Vrises
Approximate distance:	5km (3mls)
Time allowance:	1hr 45mins.

This 5 kilometres tour of the plateau may need patience with fencing and gates. It is a good infill walk if you have time to spare before returning to Chania.

Directions

From Askyfou, Ammoudari village *plateia* walk south on the main road past the cemetery and a memorial to historic battles of the struggle for independence against the Turks. Turn left down the asphalt road to Goni, but at the first bend keep straight on through a hamlet of mainly local holiday homes and then bear left down a track to a white shrine. Turn left for Goni, in view on its rocky knoll.

At Goni, turn sharp right for the road end. Follow an old lane (left of a house marked '20') through to an asphalt road and well-preserved threshing floor. (Note the large ruined house just above, once a fine specimen of the Sfakiot vernacular.) Turn left, heading north, and then turn right to leave the road on footpaths, through wire gates, up to the saddle, north of the fort. A shepherds' road serves the hilltop and ruined fort (called the 'Gou-leh') and barracks. From this viewpoint note the way to Kares ('Ka-REZZ') and also the central track back to Ammoudari. From Kares, direct routes back to Ammoudari tend to be blocked-off so it is probably easier to get back to Ammoudari on the central track.

Walk 20. Askyfou to Imbros

Grade:	A
Starting point:	Ammoudari, Askyfou (790m/2,591ft)
Finishing point:	Imbros (800m/3,046ft)
Access:	KTEL Sfakia bus or taxi from Hora Sfakion, Vrises or Askyfou
Approximate distance:	5km (3mls)
Time allowance:	1hr 30mins.

This is a walkers' short cut to Imbros on the route of the old road.

Directions
Follow Walk 19 as far as the white shrine and then keep south to meet the main road at a T-junction with a battered road sign marking the road to Akones, Asfendos and Kallikratis.

Sfakiot men are keen on owning guns ('if anyone threatens Crete, we aren't going to wait for Athens to tell us what to do'). Road signs are inevitably used for target practice. Tourists are never involved and guns, as though by common agreement, are kept low profile in the tourist season.

After about 5 minutes on the main road to Imbros (in view) leave it to the left, on the short cut offered by one of the last remaining long sections of the old road.

Imbros (800m) is claimed to be the highest village in Crete, although it is not inhabited in winter. The community has another village, Skaloti, on the south coast. In summer Imbros benefits from the cool breezes funnelled up the Imbros Gorge, making it a popular lunch spot for Samaria day tour coach drivers with time to spare on the journey to Hora Sfakion. The KTEL Sfakia schedule gives easy access to the Imbros Gorge trailhead and there is a steady demand for refreshments, breakfasts and so on.

Walk 21. The Imbros Gorge

Grade:	B
Starting point:	Imbros (800m/2,624ft)
Access:	KTEL Sfakia bus or taxi from Hora Sfakion
Finishing point:	Kommitades (200m/760ft)
Access:	Taxi from Hora Sfakion
Height loss:	600m (1,968ft)
Approximate distance:	5km (3mls)
Time allowance:	2hrs.

As a walking route, this 5-kilometre-long gorge is the most popular gorge after Samaria and also the alternative option if Samaria is closed. Unlike gorges further west, which have perpendicular cliffs, the Imbros has steep, thin spurs. Several areas of deep shade along the way make this a good midsummer walk, but there are no springs, and only one ancient well. Halfway down, a refreshment kiosk may be open.

Arriving by KTEL bus: three tavernas feature along the road south of the village, each on starting points for the walk. Unless these stops offer a less crowded start, Imbros village proper is probably best. On foot from Askyfou: continue south to the *plateia* with its three tavernas (one under refurbishment in 1998), bus stop and WCs.

Directions

Leave the *plateia*, left, down a track to the dry stream bed of the valley where splintered footpaths head south, straight for the gorge. After about 2 hours 25 minutes, with the main road in sight below, leave the gorge bed westwards via a walled mule track heading for tavernas, and Kommitades village on the main road.

Walk 22. Kommitades to Hora Sfakion

Grade:	A
Height loss:	200m (656ft)
Approximate distance:	4km (2.5mls)
Time allowance:	1hr 15mins.

Directions

(Hora Sfakion is called 'Sfakia' locally.) Walk west from Kommitades about 1 kilometre to join the Askyfou to Hora Sfakion main road. A large isolated taverna marks this junction and bus (request) stop. At about 15.45 the regular Chania–Hora Sfakion–Anopolis bus should be making its way down the hill. If you see it at the top you will have quite a few minutes to get to the bus stop in time. If you miss it there are other buses according to the Sfakia schedule.

Otherwise, continue down the road as far as the bed of the Sfakiano Gorge where there are gravel extraction works. Leave it on the unsurfaced track, on the west side, and head straight for a white Byzantine-style church in the distance.

This is, in effect, Upper Hora Sfakion, a ghost village long since bypassed through changed circumstances. In the path of the 1941 Allied army evacuation, villagers here must have struggled to fill hundreds of soldiers' water bottles from their household rainwater collecting cisterns. The modern water supply comes from an underground source. Village lanes, now overgrown, lead down to the road, bus park and harbour.

Walk 23. The Asfendos Gorge from Askyfou

Grade:	B
Starting point:	Ammoudari, Askyfou (790m/2,591ft)
Access:	KTEL Sfakia bus to Askyfou
Finishing point:	Ay. Nektarios (120m/3,96ft)
Access:	taxi from Hora Sfakion
Height gain:	300m (984ft)
Height loss:	880m (3,351ft)
Approximate distance:	11km (7mls)

The Askyfou plain in the Autumn (left) and Spring (below)

A walking group pauses to look at Niato Plateau and Kastro (Walk 27)

View of the Aradena gorge and its old kalderimi - mule track (Walk 35)

On the Aradena gorge Bailey bridge (Walk 35)

Time allowance:	Ammoudari to Goni: 35mins; to pass (1,000m/3,280ft): 1hr 30mins; to Asfendos (800m/2,624ft): 40mins; to Ay. Nektarios (120m/393ft): 2 hrs. Total: 4hrs 45mins.

Asfendos is a summer-only village in a quiet valley above the Asfendos Gorge, the next large gorge east from Imbros. The gorge develops below the valley as the mountains steepen, and ends at Ay. Nektarios on the south coast road, in a huge fan of scree. It is a much less visited gorge because Ay. Nektarios is about 6 kilometres from the Imbros to Hora Sfakion main road bus route, and busy Sfakia taxis may be unavailable. When planning this walk, check bus times beforehand at Hora Sfakion or Chania. The 17.30 Sfakia to Rethymnon service passes on its scenic route east, or a relief bus (for Samaria returnees) may be brought in from Frankokastello.

Directions

From Askyfou/Ammoudari *plateia*, walk 100 metres north and turn down right on a concrete-surfaced track. Follow this straight across the plateau as far as the third right-hand junction. Take this to join the asphalt road to Goni. Arriving at Goni, bear left around Goni hill: the asphalt ends at an old threshing circle. Keep straight on, past a grove of mature prickly oaks. Follow the road up the valley, heading south-east to the pass. Waymarked short cut footpaths occur here and there: 3.5 kilometres from Goni.

Start the descent to Asfendos on a well-preserved *kalderimi*. Continue on a shepherds' road with footpath short cuts, passing two cisterns. The V-shape of the Asfendos Gorge comes into view on the way down.

From Asfendos village turn east on the road to Kallikratis and, for the gorge, turn downhill to the right at the next junction. Join the old mule track, which has retaining walls on either side. About 2 kilometres down from Asfendos the coastline is in sight, shortly before the path zigzags down a steep section. Follow this main path as it descends left to pass a shepherds' hut built into the hillside. Then descend to cross and recross the dry river bed before leaving it again to the right. Keep right for the descent to Ay. Nektarios village where there are k*afeneia*.

Walk 24. Askyfou/Goni to Kallikratis

Grade:	D
Starting point:	Ammoudari, Askyfou (790m/2,591ft)
Access:	KTEL Sfakia bus or taxi from Hora Sfakion or Vrises
Finishing point:	Kallikratis (800m/2,624ft)
Access:	ongoing Walks 25a, b, c and 26
Height gain:	600m (1,968ft)
Height loss:	500m (1,640ft)
Approximate distance:	10km (6mls)
Time allowance:	Ammoundari to Goni: 35mins; Goni to watershed pass (1,300m/4,265ft): 4hrs 20mins; pass to Angathes summit (1,511m/4,921ft): 1hr 20mins; Angathes to Kallikratis: 1hr 20mins. Total: 7hrs 35mins.

The three mountain shepherding communities of Anopolis, Askyfou and Asi Gonia, were once linked by mule track, some sections of which still remain. This high mountain walk to Kallikratis ('Kally-KRAR-tezz') starts off on the mule track between Goni and Asi Gonia that climbs to a pass on the watershed of this lower, but very rugged, eastern block of the Lefka Ori.

Directions

Take Walk 19 or 23 to Goni. From the old threshing circle continue on for 4 minutes to the grove of mature prickly oaks. On the left is a ruined wall and line of young walnut trees and a faint footpath leads to the bordering thicket where a wire netting gate allows access to a plateau-perimeter mule track. Turn right and, after 4 minutes, pass through another gate. At the gate turn immediately uphill heading east and you are now launched on the old road to Asi Gonia ('As-see-gon-ya').

Splintered paths ascend through prickly oak and maple woodland to a first small valley with a barrel-vaulted cistern. Passing straight up this valley, continue to 950 metres where there is an old *mitato* and cistern served by a shepherds' road coming in from the north. This starts from the main Sfakia road some distance north of Askyfou. Do not think of it as an easy escape

Nearing the watershed pass in spring, Kastro in the background

from stony tracks as it is a very long road-tramp back to the plateau and there is no bus stop. Also, this mule track to Asi Gonia is the only easy way over the very steep plateau east rim.

A distinct footpath continues east, up the scree of the shallow gully above the cistern. Just before the watershed pass, arrive at a small, flat plain (no cistern). On entering this valley, bear right. The footpath ascends through rocks to a meadow at the top where there is a walled paddock, deep barrel-vaulted cistern and a ruined *mitato,* which has two rooms that are still weatherproof. From here, in clear visibility, Tripali (1,498m/4,915ft) is within easy reach as a round detour over various rocky ridges.

For Asi Gonia: follow the path eastwards over a pass down to another small plain with a cistern – the last water. From here on, the route is attractive at first, but eventually the rock changes and ongoing steep and loose-surfaced paths make the final descent very trying. *For Kallikratis:* settled visibility is necessary as this is on goat paths across ridges and hollows that all look the same and, therefore, you have to be able to see your destination. Start from the watershed pass with two litres of water (see Skills section, page 24).

Leave on the footpath on the south side of the paddock. It curves round to cross a small rocky valley and ascends a first low ridge. From this first viewpoint (and as if you were still at the pass) identify Angathes (1,511m/4,957ft) by taking a bearing off the summit. The shepherds' path to Kallikratis crosses a pass just north of the summit.

Find the best route across this area by taking it slowly and arrive at a distinct basin just below the peak. Ascend to the pass, east rim – or to the summit with its flat boulder field and trig point. Of all the varied elements that make up the 360° view, the great sweep of rock on Kastro's north face (Trek 3) is the most striking. From the pass, a path descends south-east to a valley from where a road leads down to Kallikratis.

Kallikratis is sited in an isolated fertile pocket high in the mountains on the border of Sfakia and the Rethymnon hills. In 1943 the community suffered a devastating Nazi reprisal for supporting a Resistance hide-out. The Memorial to this tragic event is just beyond the two-storey taverna. There are also one or two *kafeneia* in the village and it may be possible to arrange overnight accommodation indoors somewhere although sleeping kit may be needed (enquire in advance from Askyfou). The taverna has a hot shower available, thanks to its clientele of young working shepherds. Frankokastello (on the coast) has been a more obvious place in which to invest capital but shepherds, walkers and car tourers exploring the back roads, provide the village with midday trade.

Walks 25a, b, c. Connecting walks from Kallikratis

a. Kallikratis to Asfendos
Time allowance: 1hr
Approximate distance: 4km (2.5mls)

b. Asfendos to Goni, Askyfou
Height gain: 200m (656ft)
Height loss: 300m (984ft)
Approximate distance: 6.5km (4mls)
Time allowance: 2hrs 20mins

c. Asfendos to Imbros (E4 Trail)

Height gain:	300m (984ft)
Height loss:	300m (984ft)
Approximate distance:	5km (3mls)
Time allowance	2hrs.

A branch of the E4 Trail passes through Kallikratis on its way east to the Arcadi Monastery and beyond. However, for the return to Sfakia, either cross the valley north-westwards on footpaths from the taverna, or just follow the road going west.

Directions

From Asfendos: *for Askyfou:* turn up the valley heading north-west, reversing Walk 23 to Goni. *For Imbros:* ascend westwards via a short cut footpath to the road (E4 Trail), which passes Akones (NATO) listening antennae (reputed to be the largest in the Mediterranean), a site not visible from the Sfakia main road. Descend to Imbros valley via a footpath beside a watercourse on the north-east side of the valley. *For the Asfendos Gorge*, see Walk 23.

Walk 26. The Kallikratis Gorge

Grade:	B
Starting point:	Kallikratis (800m/2,624ft)
Access:	Lift from Askyfou or Imbros or on foot – Walks 24, 23 or 25
Finishing point:	Patsianos (150m/492ft)
Access:	Taxi from Hora Sfakion or Frankokastello
Height loss:	650m (2,132ft)
Approximate distance:	6km (4mls)
Time allowance:	2hrs 20mins.

A relatively undemanding route to the south coast road at Patsianos ('Pats'yan-OS'), this pretty tree-lined gorge can also be combined with the Asfendos Gorge to make a good round walk from Frankokastello.

Directions

Cross the valley to the outlying hamlet of Kataporia from where a footpath (not the road) heads south-west for the gorge. In a narrow section bordered by great cliffs, a concreted stretch suggests that this was a workaday route until quite recently. The gorge opens out further down and the track, paved in places, negotiates a large rockfall. From Patsianos turn east to Kapsodassos for the 1 hour north/south overland road to Frankokastello, a small beach resort with a fourteenth-century Venetian castle.

Walk 27. Ammoudari/Askyfou to Niato (E4 Trail)

Grade:	B
Start/Finish point:	Ammoudari/Askyfou (790m/2,591ft) – a circular walk
Access:	KTEL Sfakia bus or taxi from Vrises or Hora Sfakion
Height of Niato :	1,220m (4,002ft)
Height gain:	430m (1,410ft)
Approximate distance:	8km (5mls)
Time allowance:	Ammoudari to plateau rim (1,100m/ 3,608ft): 1hr 10mins; to Niato E4 Trail signpost (1,220m/4,002ft): 50mins. Total for ascent: 2 hrs. Descent to Ammoudari: 1hr. Total: 3 hrs. Extension: circuit to E4 Trail trailhead and last cistern: 1hr 30mins.

The Niato Plateau (1,220m/4,002ft) at the foot of Kastro, is a grazing pasture of about 2 square kilometres. Compared to Askyfou, Niato is small, but that gives it its particular character as a hospitable valley and place to camp perhaps before you climb Kastro or leave on the E4 Trail east/west traverse (Walk 28, Trek 3). Reached via the old mule track from Askyfou to Anopolis, Niato in itself makes an attractive walking destination from Askyfou.

Directions

From Ammoudari *plateia* walk west up the village road past a large cheese dairy and at the next bend keep straight on up a footpath to an animal shed and a road. Turn uphill and leave the road alongside a fenced compound on a short cut (red paint trail marker) up to rejoin the road at a drainage conduit. This is the shepherds' road to Niato.

Stones bordering the mule track blend in: find it just above the conduit. Zigzagging up through the prickly oak woods arrive after 30 minutes at a meadow bordered with maple trees. Askyfou's Ay. Pnevma chapel is seen at the top, over on the right. Continue up left, and then double back to reach the top in another 15 minutes.

Bird's eye view of Askyfou on the way to Niato

Cypress trees provide welcome shade for this birds' eye view of Askyfou, now far below, whilst contrasting with tree-dotted nearby hills, the starkly barren twin peaks of Kastro rise to the west above the rim of Niato. South, a seldom-used red-roofed EOZ refuge (locked) is sited on a hilltop.

Walk westwards for 5 minutes (marked with an E4 Trail pole) to Tavri, a small valley with a track, a new hut and a concrete water tank. Turn right to rejoin the shepherds' road from Askyfou (E4 Trail pole) and then turn left for Niato. Alternatively, for less of a walk along the road, bear left up the Tavri valley for 3 minutes to a cistern with a pump and an old cheese-making dairy, which can be used for shelter. Cont inue south on the track for 5 minutes and then turn right, westwards, up a small valley. The refuge is now ahead, up on the right – this footpath joins the refuge access road.

The refuge has no outside covered shelter or available water, but its terrace has a wall to shelter by. A cypress tree holds a nice draughty tree house sleeping platform (just the spot on a summer night). The Mt. Ida summit ridge is seen far to the east, and, through binoculars, so are two or three E4 Trail poles on the spine of Kastro's north ridge.

When you reach Niato, pause to examine the view. Across the plateau at 280° W note the distinct re-entrant in this east-facing flank of Kastro – the easiest route to the summit is up, and down, this wide gully. After skirting the plateau, the shepherds' road continues north-westwards over a small pass. The trailhead of the E4 Trail east/west route (Trek 3) is just beyond that pass. On the valley floor note a flat concrete cistern on the right in amongst clumps of thorny burnet. A tree marks a small *vothia* or sink-hole nearby that provides shelter for a brew up if a cold wind is blowing.

Follow the road round to an E4 Trail signpost with encouraging, but optimistic, timings; perhaps for EOZ members who are familiar with the routes.

For Imbros or Anopolis: turn to the south. See Walks 29 and 30. Otherwise, do not miss the novelty of walking across the plateau (just a few minutes without stones!) to reach the north-western pass. Just beyond the E4 Trail trailhead (marked with poles) the track ends at a cistern and then continues north-westwards as a footpath to another cistern under a lone, tall prickly oak. From here the rocky footpath, now under Kastro's north flank, continues to an area of huge boulders that look rather like cushions pinned down. It is worth getting as far as this just to see them. Beyond is a 'moonscape' valley, which, unlike other similar places in the mountains, is low enough in altitude to suit ancient cypress trees. It could be explored (remote: companions needed) as far as you wished, before retracing your steps to Niato.

Walk 28. The Ascent of Kastro

This is a circular walk.

Grade:	D
Start/Finish point:	Ammoudari, Askyfou (790m/2,591ft)
Access:	KTEL Sfakia bus or taxi from Vrises or Hora Sfakion
Height of Kastro:	2,228m (7,276ft)
Height gain/loss:	1,438m (4,717ft)
Approximate distance:	16km (10mls)
Time allowance:	Ammoudari to Niato (1,220m/4,002ft): 2hrs; ascent–descent circuit: 5hrs 30mins; Niato to Ammoudari: 1hr. Total: 8hrs 30mins.

Allow minimum of 9 hours for this circular walk from Askyfou and plan an early departure to make the most of the daylight hours. Plan also a choice of dates, as, if possible, you want settled weather for the summit view. If daylight hours are short, as in the late autumn when conditions may otherwise be ideal, consider an overnight camp at Niato, or the refuge. You can always hide unneeded items in the rocks until your return – but be careful to note the spot, and protect your food from goats.

Just because summit routes are largely in view from Niato, do not assume the ascent is going to be 'a doddle'. The belt of crags that must be climbed, just above the vegetated scree at the start of the route (and elsewhere at this level), forms a barrier to normal foot traffic and above it you are rather cut off. The crags will again have to be carefully negotiated on the descent: reserve energy for doing this competently. The going gets easier the higher you get, but a howling wind often affects the summit. Take daysack essentials including survival or 'bivi' bag. Unless melting snow prevails there is no water – start with a minimum of two litres of water from Niato. Suitable from June to November.

Directions

Follow Walk 27 and, from the entrance to Niato, study Kastro's east facing flank. Apart from the re-entrant also note the spurs descending to the plateau either side of it – there are alternative routes up or down these. Cross the plateau heading straight for the vegetated scree slope below the re-entrant, passing through the sparse tree belt to pick up the best footpath to the crags. Climb through the crags – if you've found the easiest route you should see signs of others having done this. Bear left at the crag top and cross over to a position more directly below the route of the descending dry watercourse. Ascend to about 1,900m (6,176ft) and then bear right, to the north-west, for the final 30 minutes to the summit.

A wide panorama of the peaks of the central massif extends to the west. To see this at its best, you have to get there early, before the sun moves round. To the south, far down below, the white two-storey Helvetia Taverna of Kambia (Anopolis) is just in sight. To the east, the Psiloritis summit ridge (Mt. Ida) rises beyond the hills of Rethymnon.

'Footpath' maps feature different routes on the eastern spurs of Kastro above Niato. Unless you have lots of daylight to spare, avoid these demanding rocky routes in favour of a return down the re-entrant.

Walk 29. Askyfou to Imbros via Trikoukia

Grade:	B/C
Starting point:	Ammoudari, Askyfou (790m/2,591ft)
Finishing point:	Imbros (800m/3,046ft)
Access:	KTEL Sfakia bus, or taxi from Hora Sfakion, Vrises or Askyfou
Height gain:	430m (1,410ft)
Height loss:	370m (1,213ft)
Approximate distance:	10km (6mls)
Time allowance:	Ammoudari to Niato: 2hrs; Niato to Trikoukia (1,160m/3,805ft): 30mins; Trikoukia to Imbros (via ridge top): 1hr 45mins. Total: 4hrs 5mins.

The mountains often attract cool breezes when the coast is very hot. This easily reached round walk on shepherds' paths in the mountains above Askyfou and Imbros makes a welcome change from gorge and coastal walks.

106

Directions

Follow Walk 27 to Niato's E4 Trail signpost. Turn left, south, on red gravel through free-standing rocks, and leave the plateau via a low pass. Follow a distinct footpath down to Trikoukia, another flat-floored plain. Bear right to find a cistern and concrete hut. Here, a road from Imbros (a long tramp) comes in from the south. *For Anopolis:* see Walk 30. *For Imbros* on footpaths: turn east along the north side of the fenced enclosure. (The fence blocks the start of the Imbros footpath.) Climb the hill beyond the fence to a disused *mitato* (with a weatherproof vaulted stone roof).

The footpath continues east, and passing through some big rocks, enters the next flat-floored plain. Bear right up to a low pass. From here choose one of two routes down to Imbros: (a) straight down, or (b) along the north/south ridge just above, for the best views.

For descent (a) follow the footpath immediately downhill to a cistern and then bear right past an old tree-surrounded threshing circle. The path loses height to a gully and then traverses to the right, south-east, before descending to the valley below, where oak trees provide shade near a deep barrel-vaulted cistern.

For descent (b) turn south up the ridge. The Akones (NATO) listening station is in view to the east. Pass a hollow to the right with a *mitato* with a good roof, but no water. Continue south near the edge of the ridge until it ends over a small valley. Descend to the valley and turn east on a footpath down a gully – this leads down to join descent (a) near some big oak trees.

Leave this valley, in which oak trees grow, heading south on a distinct footpath. A ruined hut features on the far side of the next small plain. Bear to the right and follow the footpath down to a road, on the north side of a ravine. Either take the road, or continue on a *kalderimi* descending the far side of the ravine. Approaching Imbros village, bear right for the main road and then turn left for the *plateia* and bus stop. Note that the last KTEL bus from Hora Sfakion to Chania may be packed with Samaria Gorge returnees. *For Askyfou:* reverse Walk 20: 1 hour 30 minutes. *For Hora Sfakion:* Walks 21 and 22: 4 hours.

Walk 30. Askyfou to Anopolis via Trikoukia

Grade:	C/D
Starting point:	Ammoudari, Askyfou (790m/2,591ft)
Access:	KTEL Sfakia bus or taxi from Hora Sfakion or Vrises
Finishing point:	Anopolis (600m/1968ft)
Access:	KTEL Sfakia–Anopolis bus or taxi from Hora Sfakion
Height gain:	430m (1,410ft) to Niato, followed by an undulating route to Anopolis with a basic height loss of: 630m (2,066ft)
Approximate distance:	21km (13mls)
Time allowance:	Ammoudari to Trikoukia (1,160m/ 3,809ft): 2hrs 30mins; Trikoukia to Scarfidia spring (1,1350m/3,723ft): 2 hrs; to Anopolis 2hrs 20mins. Total: 6hrs 50mins.

This walk follows the route of the old high-level mule track between Askyfou and Anopolis. New roads from Imbros/Trikoukia and Anopolis are projected to link up and replace the mule track altogether. However, an attractive section still remains (1998) although much of this walk is now on the shepherds' road at the Anopolis end.

Directions

Follow Walks 27 and 29 to Niato and Trikoukia. From the cistern turn south-west down a valley. (Lower down, this evolves as the Sfakiano Gorge, which is impassable from here.) After about 5 minutes the footpath forks to the right, ascending the west side of the valley in an easy gradient southwards – this is the old mule track to Anopolis.

Unless there are cairns, it is not always easy to see this contouring and undulating rocky route through sparse woodland, but it is there – take it slowly, keeping a lookout for one or two sharp zigzags. (If you feel you've missed it, retrace your steps and look again.)

From a fairly long, straight traverse, the ruined hamlet of Kali Lakki on the hillside below is glimpsed through the trees. Beyond, the traverse loses height to a forested spur with a small spurge-covered meadow and old terracing. At the west corner, facing downhill, note two medium-sized rocks just beside you on the right. Looking west, between the rocks, spot the mule track ascending the next ridge – look carefully, as it blends into the terrain.

From the top of this next ridge descend to join the Anopolis shepherds' road (road-head) at a *mitato* and spring called Scarfidia ('Scar-FEE-the-ah'). The spring emerges over a shallow pool of bright green waterweed. From here it is a long tramp to Anopolis, but there are good views along the way. Turn-offs to other workstations can be confusing: the through road negotiates upper ravines of the Kavros Gorge and loses height to pass another *mitato* with a spring and a vegetable-growing enclosure. The next important feature is a junction with an ascending road. This is the shepherds' road projected to eventually cross the entire range.

After that, views open up: the road continues west well clear of the gorge, and descends the mountainside in a series of long loops. There are some short cuts, but the terrain is very rough. Remains of the mule track are seen here and there, but it is not useable.

Limnia hamlet (Anopolis comprises several hamlets) is seen through the pines from the last straight descent, which ends at a bend near the foot of a steep ravine. The old mule track to the Madares is routed up this ravine (Trek 8). *For Anopolis:* follow the mule track south through pinewoods: 25 minutes to a sheep shed. Rejoin the road: 12 minutes to Anopolis *plateia*.

Walk 31. Askyfou to Vafes

This is Walk 18 in reverse.

Grade:	C
Starting point:	Kares or Ammoudari, Askyfou
Access:	KTEL Sfakia bus or taxi from Hora Sfakion or Vrises
Finishing point:	Vafes (250m/820ft)
Access:	Taxi from Vrises
Height gain:	110m (360ft)
Height loss:	650m (2,132ft)

Approximate distance: 10km (6mls)
Time allowance: to plateau rim (900m/2,952ft): 1hr 15mins; to TheKipou (800m/3,046ft): 1 hr; to Achatsikia (400m/1,312ft):1hr 45mins; to Vafes: 30mins. Total: 4hrs 30mins.

Directions

From the main Askyfou road, near the large modern red-roofed village church, take a walled stony mule track heading north, straight uphill. Alternatively, a road under construction (1998), is replacing this old route up to the hills of the plateau rim.

Beyond a small valley with a cistern, bear left, over and down to another, lower valley of the rim where there are prickly oaks and a cistern. Turn north and descend steeply to a shepherds' road. Krappis is in view to the east. Turn left for TheKipou, a clearing in the forest where there is a cistern, but no shelter. The road continues to Ay. Pnevma chapel on top of the forested hill to the north.

Take the road to the chapel but before it starts its final ascent, peel off downhill to the west (open views) on a path that loses height before bearing left, to enter a small high-level valley with old terracing. (Walk 18 uses a different path). From this point on, reverse Walk 18.

Walk 32. Krappis to Lake Kourna

Grade: B
Starting point: Krappis (500m/1,640ft)
Access: KTEL Sfakia bus or taxi from Vrises or Askyfou
Finishing point: Lake Kourna hamlet (50m/164ft)
Access: taxi from Georgioupoli
Height gain: 100m (328ft)
Height loss: 450m (1,476ft)
Approximate distance: 10km (6mls)
Time allowance: Krappis to east end of Dafnokorfes valley: 2 hrs; ruined hamlet (350m/1,148ft) to Lake Kourna: 1hr 30mins. Total: 3hrs 30mins.

Lake Kourna, a deep freshwater lake 1 kilometre across, comes as a surprise especially if you've just got used to arid mountains. Hidden away inland from the Georgioupoli main road and surrounded on three sides by steep or precipitous crags, the lake is fed by springs emerging underwater at its south-western corner. The water is used for agricultural irrigation, which means that you can swim in it.

This walk links with Askyfou because it follows the Askyfou shepherds' traditional droving route down to winter pastures around Georgioupoli. These days mountain sheep are billeted in sheds over the winter but all the older shepherding peoples of Crete remember what fun the transhumance operation used to be, with whole families travelling together along the way.

Krappis is a fertile valley with a small red-roofed church, about one third of the way down the Askyfou/Vrises road. A large taverna marks the bus stop. Very isolated, this place suits weddings and christenings when Sfakiots fire off their weaponry.

A footpath leaves the north-east rim of the Krappis valley to join a road along the valley under Dafnokorfes. From there another footpath descends steeply to the lake: there are rooms and tavernas, but no bus, the nearest (reliable) stop being at Georgioupoli. Taxis may be unavailable at busy times. Alternatively, on a trip from Askyfou to eastern Crete (travelling light) an overnight stop at Lake Kourna (good swimming) might suit very well.

Directions

Opposite Krappis taverna note the memorial to historic battles with the Turks in the defile just above (now full of scree) that was once the entrance to Sfakia.

From the church, pass a house and bear right on the footpath that runs the length of the perimeter fence of the cultivated meadows. Turn left around the end of the enclosure, and cross, heading north-east, to pick up an ascending wide, stony track that bears left for the rim of the valley. The Dafnokorfes valley, with its road from Alikampos ('Alee-kam-bos') is now in view. Follow the path going right, north-east, crossing a low hill or two on the way down to the road.

Walk east (a water tap can be found at a large ugly roadside sheep shed). At the end of the valley, an older track, on the right, serves a disused stone-built hamlet (terracing and a cistern, but poor water). This was obviously once an important stopping place on the old transhumance trail. You cannot yet see Lake Kourna – continue on the new road for a couple of minutes.

Below is a large amphitheatre-shaped descending valley, with Lake Kourna at its foot. Down this valley, in the centre, low hills at an intermediate level conceal a ruined hamlet. The footpath from the road heads down to this and the descent to the lake continues from there.

A detour: if you have time before making the descent, take a 20 minute detour to a nice picnic or camping spot beyond the old hamlet. From the cistern, keep on round the terraced area, to pick up a footpath heading east through trees. It traverses the mountainside to a final descending spur with a ruined stone hut on its east-facing side. Probably the best view ever of Lake Kourna and beyond is from this ruin, perched on a crag. The hut overlooked the old mule track, now eroded and engulfed by Spiny Broom and Jerusalem Sage. Under a huge oak tree just before the hut, note the cistern (good water) covered with logs.

Returning to the road, take the footpath that goes steeply down and then contour around the mid-level hills to the ruined hamlet. This is about halfway down to the lake. Below the hamlet, bear left to pass through some crags (one move needs care) and then descend over scree and along stony footpaths to join the road above the lake. Turn left and keep straight on for Georgioupoli or, after crossing the bridge over the exit river, turn right for Lake Kourna shore.

ANOPOLIS

Introduction
Above the precipitous south coast escarpment, on a wide shelf
backed by steeply-rising peaks of the southern Lefka Ori,
Anopolis village is made up of several small hamlets. Its south-
facing olive trees flourish here even at this altitude
(600m/1,968ft), although mountain shepherding is the main
traditional occupation. The tough lifestyle that goes with this, in
a harsh, dry, formerly inaccessible region of crags and stones, has
done a lot to mould the independent Sfakiot character, well
known throughout Greece. Personal self-esteem and a sense of
community remain strong despite the influences of tourism. You
will not encounter obsequious manners here, where fairness and
skill with money are equally respected.

Anopolis central, with its population of young families, has a
plateia with *kafeneon*, rooms (landlady speaks English) and a small
shop. Alternatively, Kostas' *kafeneon* (the KTEL bus terminus), on
the corner just west of the *plateia*, is the first choice for refreshments
of walkers arriving from Ay. Roumeli and Aradena. Anopolis, and
Ay. Ioannis further west, are on south–north mule tracks over the
mountains. A shepherds' road-cum-mule track connects with
Askyfou and various footpaths lead down to the coast.

The Anopolis bus to Chania, which departs from the *plateia*
about 06.30am, serves trailheads at Hora Sfakion, Imbros,
Askyfou, Krappis and Vrises and arrives at Chania by 9.15am –
this may suit flight departures. Returning, it departs Chania at
14.00, Vrises at 14.45 and Hora Sfakion at 16.15, arriving Anopolis
about 17.00 – every day except Orthodox Easter Sunday.

Kambia
Kambia, the last hamlet in the east, or the first one if you arrive
from Hora Sfakion, has rooms and restaurants, a bus stop (ask the
bus crew for Theodoros, ('Thay-odd-or-ross') and a bakery. Sited
near the cliff edge, Kambia's view out over the sea is enhanced by
the brilliance of the light resulting from the juxtaposition of
escarpment, sea and sky, making this an attractive spot to car
tourers and others arriving by bus or on foot.

Walk 33. Anopolis to Loutro

Grade:	B
Starting point:	Anopolis *plateia* (600m/1,968ft)
Access:	KTEL Anopolis bus or taxi from Hora Sfakion
Finishing point:	Loutro waterfront
Access:	Coastal boat service from Hora Sfakion or Ay. Roumeli
Height gain:	70m (229ft)
Height loss:	670m (2,198ft)
Approximate distance:	4km (2.5mls)
Time allowance:	Anopolis *plateia* to Ay. Katerini chapel (670m/2,198ft): 30mins; Ay. Katerini to Loutro: 1hr 30mins (joining Walk 34 on the descent). Total: 2hrs.

The little white chapel of Ay. Ekaterini, and the site of ancient Anopolis, a Dorian and then Roman town, tops the ridge enclosing the south side of the valley. The old mule track between Anopolis and Loutro passes below the chapel, and then zigzags straight down the steep escarpment to Loutro.

Directions
From the monument to Daskaloyannis (a notable revolutionary against the Turks) in Anopolis *plateia*, take the village street heading south out of the square and follow it through to the road up the ridge. When this turns south, note the boundary wall of ancient Anopolis up on the right. Just before the crest of the ridge, detour 5 minutes up to the chapel for a stupendous view of mountains, valley and coast.

Directly below is the Loutro peninsular with its harbour and Turkish castle. Far to the east Mt. Kedros can be seen bordering Messara bay with Paximada Island and, to the south, Gavdos and Gavdopoula islands are 48 kilometres out across the Libyan Sea. (Libyan shores cannot be seen, even from Gavdos.)

To the west, bounded by a wall of huge blocks, the remains of ancient streets, modest houses, and a cistern or two can be seen, covering a surprisingly large area of the ridge top. Inhabitants cannot have minded the arduous daily descent to the

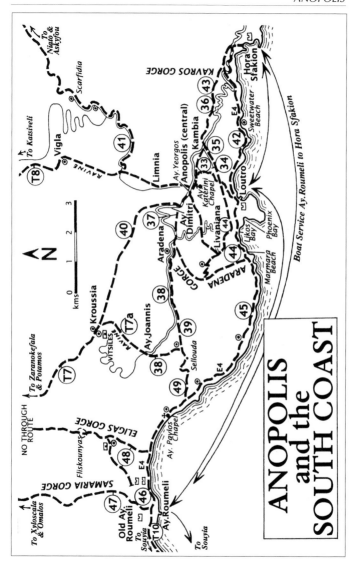

ANOPOLIS and the SOUTH COAST

fertile valley or the chill of living in such a draughty place –
unless this was a summer-only village. The basic mule track from
Anopolis to Loutro must be at least 2000 years old.

Walk 34. Kambia to Loutro

Grade:	B
Starting point:	Kambia hamlet (580m/1,902ft), Anopolis
Access:	KTEL Sfakia–Anopolis bus or taxi from Hora Sfakion
Finishing point:	Loutro waterfront
Access:	Coastal boat service
Height loss:	690m (2,263ft)
Approximate distance:	3km (1.8mls)
Time allowance:	1hr 20mins.

**From Anopolis *plateia* the path climbs the ridge, but from
Kambia where the ridge has run out, the route down is quicker.**

Arriving at the hamlet of Kambia above the escarpment

Directions

Leaving the main road beside Maria Athitaki's bakery, walk through the hamlet to the white two-storey house on (seemingly) the edge of the cliff. Here a section of walled mule track is signed to Loutro. Descend the hillside to cross a shepherds' service track, which, due to Loutro's Area of Outstanding Natural Beauty (AONB) status, soon ends. Losing height on this road, note the continuation of the old path further down, heading west towards a steeply descending gully. The path down from Ay. Ekaterini chapel joins this Kambia path.

The descending gully has a path junction: keep left for Loutro direct, or bear right into the gully for a traverse that, after 10 minutes, offers more route choices: down to Loutro via the Turkish castle or across to join the mule track up to Livaniana (Walk 44) or down to Phoenix or Likos bays.

Walk 35. Kambia to Anopolis or Ay. Ekaterini

Grade:	B
Starting point:	Kambia hamlet (580m/1,902ft)
Finishing point:	Anopolis *plateia*
Access:	KTEL Anopolis bus or taxi from Hora Sfakion
Height gain/loss:	20m (65ft)
Approximate distance:	2km (1.2mls)
Time allowance:	40mins.

The modern main road has replaced much of the valley's network of hamlet-connecting mule tracks, including the 'old road' extension of the pre-1940s road through Askyfou, Imbros and Hora Sfakion. In terms of today's recreational use a cobbled road all the way from Vrises to Anopolis and Ay. Ioannis is an intriguing thought. Much of the route can still be followed (Walks 20,21,22 and 43). In Anopolis all but a few surviving sections of old tracks are fenced off and overgrown at present. However, due to the improved water supply at Kambia, population increase has given a new lease of life to 1 kilometre of old mule track that ran the length of the valley under the escarpment ridge. The route is waymarked with red dots.

Directions

With the south-facing flank wall of the Helvetia Rooms on your right, take the concrete approach road to the house behind. Just before the house, peel off beside a fence to join a walled mule track (Kambia villagers call this 'the old road' – *pal-yoss thro-moss* in Greek), where you turn right. Keep straight on. Just after the second branch option to the right (to the main road) the old track gains height. At the top of this short hill another footpath peels off down to the right to join the main road. The mule track has lost its original surface here, but keep straight on westwards on

Anopolis in September with the ravine in Trek 8

this scenic footpath traverse above the valley. The path then loses height: pass through an unlocked wire gate and continue straight on to the road of the Ay. Ekaterini ridge. Turn up left for the chapel, or right for Anopolis *plateia*.

Walk 36. Kambia to Hora Sfakion

This is Walk 43 in reverse.

Grade:	B
Starting point:	Kambia hamlet (580m/1,902ft), Anopolis

118

Access:	KTEL Sfakia–Anopolis bus or taxi from Hora Sfakion
Finishing point:	Hora Sfakion
Access:	KTEL Sfakia bus or coastal boat service
Height gain:	20m (65ft)
Height loss:	600m (1,968ft)
Approximate distance:	4km (2.5mls)
Time allowance:	Kambia to Kavros Gorge: 1hr; to Hora Sfakion by road: 20mins; to Hora Sfakion by mule track: 45mins. Total: 1hr 20mins or 1hr 45mins.

Directions

Opposite Maria Athitaki's bakery, take the unmade road up to the top of the hill, just left of the radio masts. From here take a path (that crosses the main road lower down) and later a track straight down the re-entrant to a water hydrant. From the hydrant continue on a footpath that, after a straight section, descends to the ravine bed. Follow this down to the Kavros Gorge bed. Turn right to join the main road and then left for Hora Sfakion.

Alternatively, leave the Kavros Gorge on the *kalderimi* up the opposite side and then follow it (as a footpath) down the next hillside. A shepherds' road zigzagging up to pastures above Hora Sfakion interferes with the route of this old mule track so badly that it is easier to follow it downhill than uphill.

On the outskirts of Hora Sfakion, just beyond the first inner bend, leave the road at a telegraph pole for the short cut down to the promenade. For the KTEL bus stop, continue on the main road, turning down right to the car park, which is overlooked by a small chapel. This is the bus stop.

Walk 37. Anopolis to Aradena

Grade:	B
Start/Finish point:	Anopolis *plateia* – a circular walk
Access:	KTEL Anopolis bus or taxi from Hora Sfakion
Approximate distance:	6km (4mls)

Time allowance: Anopolis to Aradena Gorge (road): 35mins; *kalderimi* to Aradena church: 45mins; to Bailey bridge and return to Anopolis: 1 hr. Total: 2hrs 20mins.

From Anopolis the road continues west to Aradena, and Ay. Ioannis where it ends. Aradena village ('A'raTH-then-ah'), its ruined houses perched on the west side of the Aradena Gorge, near a water-collecting hollow, draws many visitors from Anopolis.

During the period of extreme privation after the Second World War, an escalating vendetta in 1947, triggered by two boys disputing the ownership of a goat's bell, obliged the community to disperse and settle elsewhere. Their descendants didn't return as the village was so cut off.

In the mid-1980s the gorge was finally spanned by a Bailey bridge, a gift to the Ay. Ioannis community from four brothers of that village who had prospered in the oil industry of Piraeus. Until then the *kalderimi* that zigzags up and down the sides of the gorge served both villages – there was no other road.

Aradena was preserved as the best 'museum of a village' Sfakia has to offer – rather to the bemusement of the locals for whom the old houses are a reminder of the 'bad old days' of hard physical toil. One or two examples of the Sfakiot vernacular in Aradena have qualified for EU-funded restoration works.

More examples of traditional house types of Sfakia can be seen (usually as ruins) in the various hamlets of Anopolis and in old Ay. Roumeli, Livaniana, upper Hora Sfakion, and Goni (Askyfou). Room width was restricted to the length of available tree trunks for beams. Wide stone-built *kamara* arches were often used to solve this problem, making two rooms side by side and, also, deep, shady front porches. First floor living rooms typically had window openings that encouraged cross ventilation, a design feature usually forgotten in today's rooming houses. Single-room houses with high ceilings had galleries either end – one as a bedroom, the other for the weaving loom beside a window, for women made cloth and the family's clothes. Most houses had a large basin for treading grapes and villages had communal flour mills and olive presses.

The Aradena Gorge and its old kalderimi (mule track)

Although the Aradena Gorge is absolutely spectacular, its massive side walls adorned with a variety of plants, it is not a popular north/south walk because unscaleable boulders block it some distance down from the bridge. The EOZ has installed two iron-ladder pitches and a hand rope that enables experienced walkers, at least, to use it as a through route, accessed via the *kalderimi*. Alternatively, footpaths from Livaniana descend into the gorge below the ladder pitches, where the route is easier (Walk 44).

The bridge offers fascinating bird's eye views of this narrow, deep gorge. Although the old *kalderimi* looks quite an undertaking, the scale is deceptive and the round walk of *kalderimi*, Byzantine church and bridge is popular with car tourers (the bridge cannot take a bus). The inspection cage is sometimes used by bungee jumpers.

Directions

From Anopolis *plateia*, walk westwards past Kostas' *kafeneon* for 10 minutes along the road to Ay. Dimitri, the most westerly hamlet of Anopolis. With the church on your right and large prickly oaks on your left, leave the road and take the concreted footpath behind the houses, turning uphill at the end. Continue

121

west, straight for the gorge, partly on a long cobbled stretch of the old road. Keep straight on across the asphalt road for the *kalderimi* or turn left along the road for the Bailey bridge.

Walk 38. Aradena to Ay. Ioannis and Sellouda

Grade:	B
Start/Finish point:	Aradena (600m/1,968ft) – a circular walk
Access:	on foot or taxi from Hora Sfakion
Height gain/loss:	200m (656ft)
Approximate distance:	11km (7mls)
Time allowance:	Aradena to Ay. Ioannis (road walk): 1hr 20mins; Ay. Ioannis to Sellouda (550m/2,094ft): 45mins; Sellouda to Aradena: 1hr 5mins. Total: 3hrs 10mins.

Before road access, Ay. Ioannis ('Eye-ee-oss Yannis) was another interesting old village. Approached on 4 kilometres of cobbled mule track, it had wall-enclosed houses separated by paved village lanes. Most of this has now gone, but the characterful *kafeneon* in the old schoolhouse makes a focal point for walkers and car tourers. A dormitory-style lodging house suits groups ascending Zaranokefala (ask for Mr. Yanni Georgidakis, 'Yor-yee-thak-is').

For the coast and Ay. Roumeli, a footpath leads down from the village to a spot called Sellouda, which is the only passable place through the cliffs (Walk 39). Alternative 'secret' routes in these forested crags do or once did exist. Some maps misguidedly promote this idea, disregarding the ravages of natural erosion and depopulation on unmaintained paths.

Directions

From the Bailey bridge, the asphalt road continues up to Ay. Ioannis: 4 kilometres. Instead, you may be able to arrange a lift from Anopolis and then walk back via Sellouda and Aradena. To do this, leave Ay. Ioannis alongside the chapel outside the village entrance gate on the footpath with red-dot waymarks, descending to the south-east. Keep on the footpath for 2 kilometres through the pine forest, downhill to a small valley with a cistern and sheepfold served by a shepherds' road. Either

Old houses in Aradena

continue on for 10 minutes beyond the valley to Sellouda, for the cliff-top view, or take the road east and then keep straight on overland to a large sheep shed below the Ay. Ioannis road. Either turn up sharp left to the road or continue on, through gates, on a surviving section of old road.

Walk 39. Aradena to Ay. Roumeli via Sellouda

This is Walk 49 in reverse.

Grade:	B
Starting point:	Aradena (600m/1,968ft)
Access:	from Anopolis Walk 37, or taxi from Hora Sfakion
Finishing point:	Ay. Roumeli
Access:	coastal boat service
Height loss:	600m (1,968ft)
Approximate distance:	11.5km (7mls)
Time allowance:	Aradena to Sellouda: 1hr 5mins; Sellouda to Ay. Pavlos: 1hr 30mins; to Ay. Roumeli: 1hr 15mins. Total: 3hrs 50mins. Starting

from Anopolis, add 45mins. Total: 4hrs
35mins.

Directions
Follow Walk 37 to Aradena and continue westwards up the Ay.
Ioannis road. Just level with the second sheep shed below the
road, descend to pick up the track from that shed. Head straight
overland about 240° SW, on a track through the pine forest.
From here, reverse the route instructions of Walk 49.

Walk 40. Anopolis to Ay. Ioannis via Kroussia

Grade:	D
Start/Finish point:	Anopolis *plateai* – a circular walk
Access:	KTEL Anopolis bus or taxi from Hora Sfakion
Height gain/loss:	640m (2,099ft)
Approximate distance:	Anopolis to Ay. Ioannis: 11km (7mls); Ay. Ioannis to Anopolis: 7km (4.3mls)
Time allowance:	Anopolis *plateia* to the top of Aradena *kalderimi*, west side: 1hr 10mins; to Kroussia (1,240m/4,068ft): 3hrs 25mins; Kroussia to Ay. Ioannis (800m/2,624ft): 1hr 15mins; Ay. Ioannis to Anopolis: 1hr 45mins. Total: 7hrs 35mins.

**Kroussia is a small upland valley in the pine forest on the Ay.
Ioannis shepherds' route to Zaranokefala and Potamos (Trek
7a). Anopolis shepherds make straight for Kroussia ('Kroos-
yah') from Ay. Dimitri hamlet (Walk 37), crossing the Aradena
Gorge via a secondary *kalderimi* about 1 kilometre further
north of the main one. (Between the two, the gorge bed has a
difficult 'waterfall' section of smooth rounded rocks.)**

**Kroussia is the focal point of this challenging 20 kilometre
circuit from Anopolis on unfrequented footpaths through
dense pine forest (companions are needed). In all
Mediterranean pine forests, fires can occur, especially in late
summer. Keep aware of your route-stage times on each section
of this walk. Escape routes would be: down – the west side of
Aradena Gorge on the eroded *kalderimi*; up – the Zaranokefala**

path from Kroussia (Trek 7a) or the shepherds' road between Kroussia and Ay. Ioannis. Take two litres of water per person from Aradena and supplement this with a brew up at Kroussia if necessary.

Directions

On the Aradena Gorge east rim, about 1 kilometre north of the main *kalderimi*, note a small 'peak'. The secondary *kalderimi* descends from behind this. The connecting ascent on the west side, however, is about 100 metres further down the gorge bed, where a distinct dip in the precipitous west rim allows this route opportunity. However, lower sections have succumbed to weather erosion. To find it, look carefully for two or three courses of low retaining wall blending into the hillside one third of the way up the correct gully. Reaching it involves a rather exposed move from one foothold on a small rock (worn white by shepherds' boots): you have to enjoy rock-scrambling for this.

As a fenced enclosure now interrupts the footpath from Ay. Dimitri, and if rock scrambling is not for you, there is an alternative route: from behind the ruined house at the top of the Aradena *kalderimi*, on the west side, follow a footpath uphill over old terracing for 15 minutes to a seriously fenced enclosure. Pass around this to the left and through an unlocked gate in another fence at the top. Turn right along the fence and, after 50 metres, pick up an ascending path that enters the pine forest. Long engulfed by trees, old terracing is now part of the forest floor. Within sight of the gorge rim and on the most likely-looking of the sheep paths, head for the first distinct valley, or dip, in the gorge west rim.

A short section in a crag leads down to this valley where a sheep path continues north, parallel to the gorge and over the next spur. Beyond the spur turn up left, west, beside it. As the spur levels out a large crag is seen rising above the forest. The path ascends left under the crag to an open valley with a large walled enclosure. Keeping straight on through the enclosure, enter a shallow gully. Continue up this to a Y-junction of paths – bear left for Kroussia, an open, flat area with three cisterns (poor water). Vitsiles *mitato* is 200 metres up the shepherds' road (from Ay. Ioannis) that enters Kroussia from the south. For the descent to Ay. Ioannis, see Trek 7.

Walk 41. Anopolis to Askyfou via Kali Lakki

This is Walk 30 in reverse.

Grade:	C/D
Starting point:	Anopolis *plateia*
Access:	KTEL Anopolis bus or taxi from Hora Sfakion
Finishing point:	Ammoudari, Askyfou
Access:	KTEL Sfakia bus, or taxi from Hora Sfakion, Vrises (or Askyfou)
Height gain:	This is an undulating route between the levels of 600m (1,968ft) and 1,220m (4,002ft), with a basic height gain of 630m (2,066ft)
Approximate distance:	21km (13mls)
Time allowance:	7hrs 40mins.

Part of the old high-level mule track between Anopolis and Askyfou still remains (1998) although shepherds' roads from each end are designed to link up. This walk is easier from Askyfou because the long road-tramp at the end is then downhill. However, if starting from Anopolis suits your itinerary, directions to the trailhead follow.

Directions

From Anopolis *plateia*, follow Trek 8 to the foot of the mountains and the mule-track ravine. After an initial long straight section, the road gains more height in wide loops, then heads north-east above the upper reaches of the Kavros Gorge to end (1998) at Scarfidia spring ('Scar-FEE-thee-ah') and *mitato*. From here turn north, uphill, bearing right, to pick up the mule track, which is more distinct nearer the crest of the hill – the first ridge on the way east. The little meadow on the forested spur west of Kali Lakki (a ruined hamlet) is now across the next re-entrant. Follow Walk 30 in reverse from there.

THE SOUTH COAST

Introduction

To walkers the gem of western Crete is the region of Sfakia ('Ss'fak-ya') with its spectacular mountain scenery and gorge-punctuated coastline free of roads from Hora Sfakion to Souyia. Coastal villages, and therefore several trailheads, are served by boat. In spring and autumn another delight is the climate – the south coast is often sunny – or at least dry – when the north coast is overcast or wet. Rocky coves with white or black-stoned beaches offer good bathing from the coastal walks that link villages, with their harbours, and gorges. Waterfront restaurants are free of the unsightly picture-menus of north-coast resorts and much of the accommodation is not pre-booked by tour operators, which allows for a flexible itinerary.

Hora Sfakion

'Village of Sfakia' is tedious to say – locals (and the bus crew) call it 'Sfakia'. This is a former fishing village at the end of the road down the steep south coast escarpment. Nowadays it is part of the Samaria Gorge round trip – ferryboats from Ay. Roumeli land passengers here by the thousand for their bus journeys back to other resorts. Much of this operation circulates east of the promenade, by a large car and bus park, leaving the rest of the village to carry on almost as normal. 'Sfakia' has supermarkets, shops selling souvenirs, books, maps, clothes and beach kits, restaurants and lots of accommodation. It is noisy, with late night dining and a discotheque operates in midsummer. The community has shelved the idea of public WCs, given the potential numbers of users, and instead the coffee bars and restaurants share this service. The harbour beach below the promenade and the town beach on the west side of the village are good for swimming.

After the Battle of Crete, thousands of Allied soldiers were evacuated under heavy bombardment from Hora Sfakion harbour by the Royal Navy between 28 and 31 May 1941. Old shells sometimes feature as house embellishments in Loutro and Anopolis. The operation was organised from a cave – perhaps the big cave (with a disused chapel inside) just above the road to Anopolis. If you have time to spare, climb up to it for an alternative view of the whole modern set-up below – or take the mule track up the next hillside heading east, to an old hamlet in a small pine wood. There are good views also from the village waterworks in the thirteenth-century Venetian castle, just above the bus park.

A bus departs 07.00 daily (and at other times) providing walkers with access to trailheads inland at Imbros or Askyfou.

Loutro

As they are sheltered natural harbours, Loutro and nearby Phoenix bay, which has springs, have often been mentioned in the history of Mediterranean seafaring. Loutro has been a Roman port, a Venetian harbour, a community of seafaring merchants, a Sfakiot pirates' lair, and a Turkish stronghold. Today, in total contrast, it is a mildly upmarket tourist resort and an EU Area of Outstanding Natural Beauty (AONB).

Fortunately, thanks to the difficulty of making roads to Loutro, oil tanker moorings were established at Kali Limenes in eastern Crete, rather than here. This was relatively recently, although before today's tourism was even imagined. AONB status should save Loutro bay from road-cutting for the foreseeable future. Loutro has supermarkets and shops selling souvenirs, books, clothes, and beach kits, restaurants and lots of accommodation. A boat-taxi supplements the regular boat schedule.

The old mule track that zigzags up the steep escarpment directly above Loutro gets the sun all day, making it a hot walk if there are no breezes. See Walks 33 and 34.

Walk 42. Hora Sfakion to Loutro (E4 Trail)

Grade:	B
Starting point:	Hora Sfakion
Access:	KTEL Sfakia bus or coastal boat service
Finishing point:	Loutro
Access:	coastal boat service
Height gain/loss:	This is an undulating coastal walk.
Approximate distance:	6km (4mls)
Time allowance:	2hrs (either way).

Returning from Marmara Beach to Loutro (Walk 44)

Leaving Potamos in late May (Trek 6 - in reverse)

At Roussies (Trek 8), Trocharis in the background

View east from Pachnes summit as the shadows begin to lengthen (Trek 9)

In terms of walks, this rugged, but well-tramped, varied stretch of coastal footpath between two popular centres surely qualifies as a Mediterranean classic, with good bathing along the way.

Loutro to Hora Sfakion may be preferred because 1.5 kilometres on the main road then comes at the end as a welcome change from the rocky footpath. Boat ticket kiosks: Hora Sfakion – along the promenade; Loutro – centre of the beach (ask which jetty).

Looking eastwards towards Sweetwater beach

Directions

Leave Hora Sfakion up the village street behind and parallel to the promenade. Turn right up some steps and follow a village lane to reach the main road. Turn left, west and walk past the Kavros Gorge (above a beach) to the first uphill bend: 1.5 kilometres. The footpath (E4 Trail) from the vehicle crash barrier, loses height to negotiate a large rock buttress, a section of footpath hacked out of the cliff. A short part of this feels a little exposed as the sea is directly below.

Descend through a big rockfall to Sweetwater Beach. The west part of the rockfall is fairly recent (follow the cairns) and it is dangerous to camp on the beach directly under the cliff – anyone who does hasn't seen what it looks like from the boat! As the name denotes, fresh water, collected in hollows made by bathers and campers, emerges on this stony beach. (Water from here serves Loutro by underwater pipe.) In summer, a small refreshments bar on a rock operates on bottled gas.

The footpath continues over the next promontory and, after passing small bays, gains height to avoid Loutro's rocky shoreline. Enter the village through a goat gate. The churchyard, with its benches, provides quiet shade away from the busy waterfront.

The route in reverse: the coastal footpath can be seen from Loutro waterfront – just filter through the end houses: painted arrows mark the way.

Walk 43. Hora Sfakion to Anopolis

This is Walk 36 in reverse.

Grade:	B
Starting point:	Hora Sfakion
Access:	KTEL Sfakia bus or coastal boat service
Finishing point:	Anopolis (600m/1,968ft)
Access:	KTEL Sfakia–Anopolis bus, or taxi from Hora Sfakion
Height gain:	600m (1,968ft)
Approximate distance:	4km (2.5mls)
Time allowance:	2hrs 45mins.

The Historical Museum in Heraklion displays a photograph of the old cobbled road to Anopolis and the hillsides above Hora Sfakion, pre-1950s before the new road was made. Parts of it near Hora Sfakion, east of the Kavros Gorge, are now rather difficult to follow, but west of the gorge the old road is more clearly routed up a narrow ravine just behind the hill of the modern road. Walkers reach the top just to the right of the radio masts on the skyline.

Directions

Follow Walk 42 to the Kavros Gorge and then turn up the stony gorge bed. In a few minutes note the retaining wall of the *kalderimi* descending the eastern side. The continuation of this track, westwards, is routed up the tributary ravine opposite. Just a few traces of paved track remain in the lower part.

Above Hora Sfakion (Walks 36 and 43)

When the ravine becomes shallow and opens out, take an undemanding ascending footpath out of it to the right, which leads to a track by a water hydrant. The track is the route of an underground pipe up to the radio masts. On reaching this point on the skyline, either bear left for Kambia hamlet (rooms and restaurants) or right for a track to the main road further west – and from there Anopolis *plateia* is about 1 kilometre away.

Walk 44. Loutro to Livaniana and Marmara Beach

Grade:	B
Start/Finis point:	Loutro – a circular walk
Access:	coastal boat service
Height gain:	300m (984ft)

Height loss:	300m (984ft)
Approximate distance:	9km (5.5mls)
Time allowance:	Loutro to Livaniana (300m/984ft): 1hr 35mins; Livaniana, Aradena Gorge – Marmara Beach: 2 hrs; to Loutro: 45mins. Total: 4hrs 30mins.

Livaniana's depopulated state and isolated location on the steep, rocky hillside above Phoenix and Likos bays made it the last village of Sfakia to get a road – the junction for this is beyond Anopolis, just before the Aradena Gorge bridge. Walkers can follow sections of old mule track to Livaniana either from Anopolis or Phoenix Bay. On several maps this village is called 'Livadiana'.

Livaniana has old terracing above the Aradena Gorge and from there two footpaths descend to the gorge bed below the rockfall with the iron-ladder pitches (Walk 37) making a good circular walk: Loutro, Livaniana, Marmara Beach and then back to Loutro on the coastal path.

Directions
Follow Walk 45 as far as the hill beyond Phoenix Bay where there is a chapel and palm trees. Note the steep gully in the hillside east of Livaniana ('Lee-van-yan-ah'): a well-built zigzagging *kalderimi* is routed up this. Turn uphill here to join the *kalderimi* via a gate and a short car track.

Livaniana's new road, bulldozed down from the top of the escarpment, has cut out the last section of the *kalderimi* where it once entered the village. Now clamber over rocks to join this road.

At this point on the outskirts of Livaniana, note two old houses with earthen (clay mix) roofs, the local roofing material until concrete became available in the 1950s. These roofs needed re-laying annually to be effective. In wet places like Askyfou they leaked after prolonged rain, a discomfort still not forgotten by those who experienced it.

A modern *kafeneon* overlooking the view of the coast, now far below, contrasts with an old village cistern alongside it. Make your way up to the white church at the top of the village and then continue over a large rock to the crest of the ridge. There is a water tap just before the rock. The Aradena Gorge and old terracing is now in view; you have a choice of routes from here.

For Anopolis: walk north along the ridge until you come to a *kalderimi* that, supported by its retaining walls, ascends a steep crag (you cannot see it at first). Once above the crag the *kalderimi* crosses a new road, heads for the top of the Anopolis ridge to the north-east, and then descends via the hamlet of Ay. Georgos, just a few minutes from Anopolis *plateia*. (See Walk 33 for the return to Loutro.)

For Marmara Beach or Aradena: two paths descend into the gorge. The first, which is steep, is waymarked with dots and descends almost immediately; the second, which is easier, leaves from the white chapel in the far distance across the terracing. Head for this chapel on various paths at the back of the terracing, and then from the chapel, follow a distinct footpath down, heading north-west over more spurge-covered terraces. Birds indicate the whereabouts of a spring emerging beside the path, under a rock. A tiny pool collects in a log.

For Aradena: at the gorge bed turn up right for the iron-ladder section: 20 minutes (Walk 37). *For Marmara Beach:* bear left, through large boulders, for the footpath down the gorge.

A panoramic view of Loutro harbour

Loose stones in the gorge bed make walking down far easier than walking up, although it is scratchy in places. Various rockfalls have to be negotiated – cairns normally indicate the best routes through these. Another small spring emerges in the largest rockfall. Take no risks – if you have to do any real rock scrambling, you haven't found the easiest way down – return and look again.

Mature pines provide shade here and there. In summer, as the gorge bed levels out lower down, purple oleander contrasts with the rich yellow ochre of the massive perpendicular walls. In spring the endemic Cretan ebony, a chasmophyte with clusters of purple flowers, billows out from the walls just before the gorge ends at Marmara Beach, a crag-sided inlet with turquoise water and deep pools.

Walk 45. Loutro to Ay. Roumeli

Grade:	B
Access:	Coastal boat service
Height loss/gain:	This is an undulating coastal walk
Approximate distance:	14km (9mls)
Time allowance:	Loutro to Marmara Beach: 45mins; Marmara to Ay. Pavlos chapel: 3hrs; to Ay. Roumeli: 1hr 15mins. Total: 5hrs.

A necessary alternative to boat transport, and now part of the E4 Trail, this 12 kilometres coastal path is well-tramped and easy to follow. On one stretch there is not much shade and there is none at midday on Marmara Beach. Plan your water supply: the south coast can be very hot.

Directions

Take the lane behind Loutro Beach kiosk. Bear left through the goat gate above the church and follow a footpath up to the Turkish castle. Keeping west, bypass Phoenix Bay (chapel and palm trees) and then follow a paint-waymarked path down through rocks to Likos Bay (rooms and tavernas) where the footpath passes across the terrace of Niko's taverna and rooms.

Crags and a large cave border the western end of the beach. Climb up here to rejoin the footpath that traverses above the crags and then descends to Marmara Beach (Aradena Gorge). The taverna and overnight cabins here may operate only at busy times of year.

Picking up the footpath again, ascend the crag at the rear of the beach and then climb steadily to get above the next sea cliffs. A 'remote' 4.5 kilometre section follows, with very little shade. A shepherds' concrete cistern lies below the footpath, about halfway along. Beyond it, in the cliff above, note the white droppings of griffon vultures: this undisturbed spot is their roosting place. If there is a carcass lying in the mountains, six or eight of these birds (the 'Car-na-vee') will be circling above it.

The bare headland ends and the path descends a crag into pine forest. Pass a concrete-topped cistern and, in 10 minutes, the junction with the Sellouda trail (Walk 48), in a long shady stretch with pine needles underfoot. From this point it is 20 minutes to Ay. Pavlos chapel with its spring and small taverna opposite a lone rock in the sea.

Ay. Pavlos

The restored chapel marks the spot where St. Paul the Evangelist is reputed to have landed on his ill-fated expedition from Myra (Demre, Turkey) to Rome in October AD 59. October was too late in the year for an easy voyage and his ship was blown off course several times before finally being wrecked at Malta.

On a good year Ay. Pavlos spring may run into midsummer, but on the other hand it may not. Early in the year, with your back to the chapel look about 15 metres to the left. As the waves roll back, a distinct freshwater stream runs out over the stones. (The taverna may now use much of this water supply.)

All along this coastline tiny springs, associated with the snow-melt, line the water's edge in the early spring, but they are seen only on rare occasions when the sea is very still. A larger one, of (unfit) brackish water below the Eligas Gorge is used after dark by goats and other animals of that gorge.

Climb the sand dune behind the taverna to rejoin the coastal path. In 25 minutes pass the entrance to the Eligas Gorge and then descend over dunes to a long stony beach. Gain height again, through rocks at the western end, and then finish by crossing the last promontory, the site of ancient Tara, a Dorian city.

Ay. Pavlos, and the way to Ay. Roumeli

Ay. Roumeli, its heliport protected from wave erosion by precast concrete Staybits, is across the Samaria River just below. On a good year the river runs well into the summer. Camping is normally allowed under the trees at its estuary. Green algae grows on seashore stones wetted by river water.

Ay. Roumeli

Ay. Roumeli new village does a busy refreshments and lunch trade with tour groups walking the Samaria Gorge, finishing up here to be taken off by boat perhaps after a quick swim. The boat service includes two large landing craft, 'Samaria' and 'Daskaloyannis', able to dock even when the sea is rough. After the last boat has left, Ay. Roumeli settles down to the relaxed atmosphere only a place without roads can have and thus it is popular with walkers and with Greek holidaymakers, particularly in August. There is good swimming from the gravelly black-stoned beach that, like Souyia, shelves away fairly quickly. This is a fiercely hot place at times – sunbeds can be hired. Apart from restaurants and rooming houses, there are supermarkets and shops selling souvenirs, beach kits and books. Noise: (the sound of the sea) but also, a discotheque might operate in midsummer (enquire).

136

Ay. Roumeli old village, at the head of the wide valley behind the first spur of the gorge, has two outlying chapels that make focal points for short walks. Turkish forts and the nearby Eligas Gorge make more demanding day walks. The Samaria Gorge itself is a useful passage to the Omalos Plateau and, westwards, is the challenging two-day coastal footpath to Souyia (Trek 10). The boat service provides transfers (or excursions) to other coastal villages, and the Post Office mailboat (ten-passenger capacity) between Paleochora and Gavdos Island may stop for 5 minutes here, once a week (enquire).

Walk 46. The Gorge of Samaria

This is Walk 2 in reverse.

Grade:	B
Starting point:	Ay. Roumeli
Access:	coastal boat service.
Finishing point:	Xyloscala (1,250m/4,101ft)
Access:	KTEL Omalos bus or taxi from Chania
Height gain:	1,250m (4,101ft)
Approximate distance:	18km (11mls)
Time allowance:	Ay. Roumeli to Iron Gates: 1 hr; Iron Gates to Samaria old village (330m/1082ft): 1hr 40mins; to Xyloscala: 4 hrs. Total: 6hrs 40mins.

Directions

Leave Ay. Roumeli at 7am and you will not meet descending walkers until about 11am. Alternatively, time it so that you leave Samaria old village at 2pm and the rest of the walk up to Xyloscala will be relatively undisturbed.

Walk 47. Around Ay. Roumeli

Grade:	A/B
Start/Finishing point:	This is a circular walk from Ay. Roumeli.
Access:	Coastal boat service

Height gain:	100m (328ft)
Approximate distance:	3km (1.8mls)
Time allowance:	Ay. Roumeli up to the Turkish fort: 45mins; down to old Ay. Roumeli and return: 45mins. Total: 1hr 30mins. Add extra for detours.

As seen from Ay. Roumeli old village, the Turkish fort on the spur at the end of the valley features dramatically on the skyline. Mule tracks served the fort on both sides of the spur and a circuit on these offers interesting views of both new and old villages. The weather-eroded south-facing slope is best tackled as the ascent.

Directions

From Ay. Roumeli main street, take the gorge-approach path as far as the Byzantine chapel. The 30 minute-long ascent footpath starts just behind it. Battered by winter storms, there is not much left of the mule track this side, but on the northern side a more distinct route descends to old Ay. Roumeli. Above the fort, the razed remains of what was presumably a signalling post feature further up the spur, and at the very top, a trig point marks the summit of Piskopos (885m), the last peak of the Volakias ridge. Return down the same way you came up. The ascent and descent of Piskopos, although within sight of everything going on down below, is very unfrequented and also very demanding on the knees. Take daysack essentials: a minimum of two litres of water, a whistle and a torch.

The footpath up to the little chapel in the valley's east rock face is reached from behind the old schoolhouse. Disused, the chapel's *panayeri* (Saint's day festival) is in January, when the Ay. Roumeli community is nowadays in Chania. Opposite, above the village to the west, on the spur descending from Piskopos, is another small white disused chapel. Heading for this, take the footpath across the bridge and turn sharp left at first, as if for the fort, before doubling back and up. The picturesque Ay. Roumeli church beside the gorge main trail remains very important to the local community.

Walk 48. The Eligas Gorge

Grade:	C/D
Start/Finishing point:	Ay. Roumeli – a circular walk
Access:	Coastal boat service
Height gain:	(a) to Turkish forts 600m (1,968ft); (b) to Fliskounyas 700m (2,296ft)
Distance:	(a) 9 kilometres (5.5 miles); (b) 10 kilometres (6 miles)
Time allowance:	Ay. Roumeli to Eligas Gorge: 45mins. (a) to Turkish forts: 2hrs 30mins; to Ay. Roumeli: 1hr 50mins. Total: 5hrs 5mins. (b) to Fliskounyas: 2hrs 45mins; to Ay. Roumeli: 1hr 50mins. Total: 5hrs 25mins.

Far higher than Ay. Roumeli fort, on top of the eastern spur of the gorge exit, are two more ruined forts. One is seen from the beach; both from the ferryboat. Few people make the effort to get up to this thought-provoking eagles' eyrie of a site, perched on a thin ridge above two completely contrasting gorges, one an unfrequented haven for wildlife, the other a top money-earning National Park.

The Eligas Gorge ('El-LEE-gas') itself has an unusual feature: one third of the way up, scree fans descending on both sides dam the gorge, forming a fairly deep, humid basin called Flee-skoun-yas. Ancient terracing and varied trees make up its tangled, but passable floor. Beyond it, some maps show a footpath through to the high mountains, but this is misleading. The top, 7 hours effort from Ay. Roumeli, including 4 hours above the humid basin, ends at 1,300m (4,226ft) in crags impassable to non-rock climbers. A cistern on the route up to the forts is the only available water, as fort cisterns are disused. This gorge is seldom visited, in spite of its proximity to Ay. Roumeli. Take daysack essentials from the entrance to the gorge: a minimum of two litres of water, a whistle and a torch.

Directions

Follow Walk 49 to the Eligas Gorge. A distinct footpath leads up the gorge through sparse pine forest and over scree. After about 20 minutes, the path bears left in the gorge bed to an old sheepfold and a crag with a shepherds' cave. *For the two Turkish forts* (and the usable cistern) turn up left of the crag to pass the cistern within a few minutes, on top of a first small spur (view). The path gains height and heads south to Angelokampi, an area of spurge-covered old terracing, directly above the coastal cliffs. The footpath continues steeply up through sparse pine forest. Although Angelokampi seems high, it is only about one third of the way up to the ridge top. But the pull is well worth it, just to visit this remarkable site. Turkish garrisons of Sfakia used trumpeters to pass messages to one another.

For Fliskounyas and beyond (remote: companions needed) follow the footpath up the gorge and over the dam formed by the scree. Beyond the basin, the gorge narrows considerably and the tree-shaded route is rocky and steep. The gorge opens out at the top, its bed littered with trees swept down by thawed snow, to end in a 'waterfall' crag worn smooth by the snow-melt of millennia. The tricky pitch that stops non-rock climbers is on the left. If you have planned to tackle this (with climbing equipment) treat this as a trekking expedition, but take enough water for a downhill return if necessary. See Treks 7, 5a, 6a for ongoing routes.

Walk 49. Ay. Roumeli to Anopolis via Sellouda

This is Walk 39 in reverse.

Grade:	B
Starting point:	Ay. Roumeli
Access:	coastal boat service
Finishing point:	Anopolis (600m/1,968ft)
Access:	KTEL Anopolis bus or taxi from Hora Sfakion
Height gain:	600m (1,968ft)
Approximate distance:	14km (9mls)
Time allowance:	Ay. Roumeli to Ay. Pavlos chapel: 1hr 15mins; to path junction: 20mins; to Sellouda cliff top (595m/1,952ft): 2hrs 20mins; to Aradena: 1hr 5mins; to Anopolis (via bridge): 45mins. Total: 5hrs 45mins.

From Ay. Roumeli waterfront, note the forested escarpment east and the distinct long descending crag between the forest and

the bare rocky headland. On the skyline, a little distance in front of this crag, there is a patch of red rock: this is Sellouda. Easy-to-manage scree slopes are at their highest there and so the mule track to Ay. Ioannis, Aradena and Anopolis was routed up through the cliffs at that point. Such is the orientation of the escarpment that if you leave Ay. Roumeli at 7am the climb can be done in the shade. Mention Sellouda in Ay. Roumeli – it is a route that has given pleasure to countless walkers over the years, but a road is threatened.

Water
Of villages above the escarpment, Ay. Ioannis (*kafeneon*) is 2 kilometres off the main Aradena to Anopolis footpath and linked to Aradena by 4 kilometres of asphalt road. There are no other *kafeneia* or tavernas en route (1999) before Anopolis *plateia* is reached (a new *kafeneon* is projected for Aradena – enquire). Cisterns beyond the cliff top have poor water. (A marginally better one is beside the Aradena Bridge.) Plan your water needs at Ay. Roumeli. Contingency: if the taverna at Ay. Pavlos is closed and the spring at the water's edge is not running, there is a cistern beside the footpath, 10 minutes east of the Sellouda path junction (Walk 45). Many walkers arrive at the top of the Sellouda trail seriously dehydrated through not having allowed enough water for the ascent-effort on a hot day – and at that point they are still some distance from good water.

Directions
Ideally leaving at 7am, cross the Samaria River bed, picking up a section of mule track, on the left, over the Tara promontory. The coastal footpath (E4 Trail poles) is well tramped. The main effort is the long stony beach 25 minutes from Ay. Roumeli.

Take the footpath up the sand dune at the end of the long stony beach (passing the Eligas Gorge entrance). A pleasant forested section follows. Descend over sand dunes to Ay. Pavlos taverna and chapel. Pause here no longer than 20 minutes if you want shade on the Sellouda ascent, and then, on the other side of the chapel, turn up sharp left to regain the footpath through the forest. After 20 minutes arrive at the path junction (paint signs). *For Loutro* keep straight on (3.5 hours). *For Sellouda, (Ay. Ioannis/Anopolis)* bear left uphill.

Ascend the path through pine forest and cross the scree of a ravine bed. Continue up the path from the opposite bank on easy zigzags. Fortunately, whatever the time of day, trees provide shade at intervals. Finally, above the scree, a paved *kalderimi* ascends through the crags to the cliff top. Sellouda, with its shady trees and panoramic view of the coastline is a favourite picnic spot with walkers. Lammageiers from the Samaria Gorge glide past this cliff top so often at midday on their foraging trips that it is well worth keeping a look out for them.

Head north-east on a walled mule track, past old terracing. Here are pine forested and very stony undulating hills under the southernmost peaks of the Lefka Ori. On the left, Zaranokefala (2,100m/6,889ft) towers behind Ay. Ioannis – a single white chapel above the trees marks the location of this village. Follow the footpath down to a hollow with a sheepfold and cistern (poor water) served by a shepherds' road. *For Ay. Ioannis:* take the footpath heading north-west up from the sheepfold. *For Aradena/Anopolis:* follow the road east through the pinewood (Walk 38).

Enjoying a break at Sellouda

CHAPTER 4

MOUNTAIN TREKS

Introduction
These treks are backpacking routes that need three days or more
– either camping or bivouacking kit, and water and food supplies
have to be carried. Some treks are shown on maps as branches of
the E4 Trail, but not all of these are waymarked.

The mountains are always snow-covered in winter – it forms
the all-important water supply of the region. In Spring,
snowdrifts may render summit ascents and traverses of high
steep slopes dangerous to walkers – it all depends, as long-lasting
drifts shaped by blizzards vary each year. South-facing
mountainsides are free of snow sooner than the sheltered high
valleys and the northern slopes. Most trekking routes over the
range are normally possible by early May, but do not set your
heart on any particular summit ascent in the central massif before
mid-June. This guide aims to offer route options to suit the
conditions you find.

All treks in the mountains that rise to over 2,400m (7,880ft)
and attract all weathers – including long hours of relentless
sunshine – need careful advance planning. Needless to say, help
to conserve the beauty of this (beleaguered) wilderness by
carrying away all your rubbish.

The Madares
Above the tree line the mountains are desert-like in character
although in places tiny nutritious plants on the barren terrain
sustain large numbers of sheep brought up in June from the
foothill villages. These high-level pastures are called the Madares
('Ma-THAR-res'). Before service road access was built, shepherds
using mules worked in shifts at their family *mitatos* ('mee-tat-
toes'), making cheese on the spot. Every working *mitato* had
living quarters, a water supply, a cheese-making set-up and a
cheese store – for the cheeses matured for a month before,
wrapped in straw, they could be brought down by mule.
Workaday mule tracks served the high mountains and trekkers

can still enjoy sections of these that have escaped the road-making programme.

Valleys of the Central Massif

Three high-level valleys in the heart of the range serve as crossroads for footpaths and mule tracks. The Livada valley (1,800m/5,904ft) is the true crossroads of the old mule track routes shown on almost all maps of Crete. However, new roads and the location of Kallergi Refuge (Omalos) have made the Katsiveli valley (1,940m/6,364ft), with its EOZ mountain refuge, more frequented by walkers than Livada. Both Katsiveli and Livada are small *oropethia* – mountain plains – similar to Omalos and Askyfou. The Potamos valley (1,750m/5,689ft) is the third crossroads, but this valley is different, being long and narrow as its name, 'river', suggests. Orientated north/south it evolves as the Eligas Gorge, the next gorge east of Samaria.

Various through routes and escape routes can be planned around the options presented by these three crossroads valleys. Remotest are the trails to and from Livada, the area least threatened by road-making (note that on some maps, Livada is wrongly named 'Klissida').

Trek 1. Theriso to Livada via Kolokithas

Grade:	D
Starting point:	Theriso (600m/1,968ft)
Access:	Taxi from Chania
Finishing point:	Livada cistern (1,800m/5,905ft)
Access:	Ongoing from Treks 2a, 3a, 4
Height gain:	to valley rim (1,900m/6,233ft), 1,300m (4,265ft)
Approximate distance:	16km (10mls)
Time allowance:	Theriso to Alyakes spring (850m/2,788ft): 1hr 35mins; to Mono Scarfidi spring (1,080m/3,543ft): 1hr 15mins; to Selya spring (1,360m/4,461ft): 1hr 30mins; to Kapsekas spring (1,600m/1,968ft): 1hr 50mins; to Kolokithas *mitato* (1,800m/5,905ft): 1hr 30mins; to Livada cistern: 1hr 30mins. Total: 9hrs 10mins.

This is the northern section of the ancient north/south mule track over the mountains between Theriso and Anopolis, which winds its way through the Madares by the easiest means possible. Although this northern approach is well-supplied with springs, it is little-used by trekkers who tend to be drawn at first to Omalos (Kallergi Refuge) and branches of the E4 Trail. Starting conveniently near Chania, the total ascent is 1,300m (4,265ft).This is 370m (1,214ft) more than the E4 Trail over Melindaou summit, and there is one short extra route stage to Katsiveli (Trek 4). However, the main difference from Trek 6 (E4 Trail) is that this is a far less frequented route.

This trek suits from early May if west-facing mountainsides below 1,800m (5,905ft) are free of snow. Ongoing routes from Livada in the spring could be limited to Treks 2a, 4, 8a and 6a. Take food for two and a half or three days.

Arrive at Theriso ('TH'EH-riss-oh') road-end by a monument to Eleutheros Venizelos, the Cretan lawyer and statesman who achieved union for Crete with the Greek nation in 1913. A taverna lunch or dinner here may suit a late start – perhaps to camp at one of the springs.

Theriso lies in a valley between two long low ridges typical of the northern foothills. The shepherds' road is routed along the top of the east ridge and by following this at first you are able to get on to the mule track at 1,180m (3,871ft).

Directions

From the Venizelos monument, walk 1 minute back towards the village. Turn down right by a new two-storey house. Cross a small stream bed and bear right on an uphill footpath – a short cut to the road. Turn right at the first road and then almost immediately left at a junction. At the ridge top the road forks: east is for Drakona and Kambi; south is for the mountains – follow this along the ridge.

Assisted by soil-retaining ancient terracing, 500-year-old plane trees cling to the steep crag at the head of the valley. The first spring-served trough, named Alyakes ('Al-ya-kez') emerges in this shady woodland. *For Zourva:* (45 minutes) a footpath continues west from the spring, across a meadow, and down to the next low ridge. *For Kolokithas,* the road starts to climb: in about 40 minutes reach an open, bracken-filled valley (990m/3,248ft).

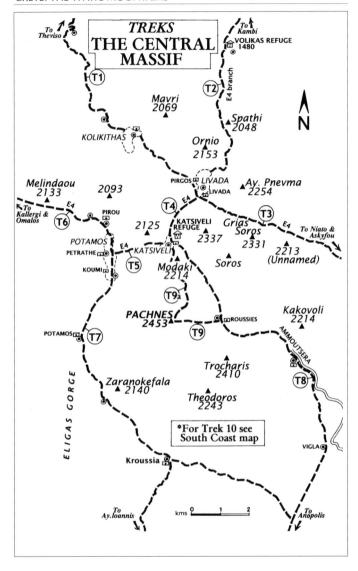

From this, take an uphill short-cut footpath south-east to avoid road-loops. On rejoining the road, bear right and climb the opposite bank to find Mono Scarfidi spring-served trough in a grove of Plane and Walnut trees.

Either follow the road west from the spring, or continue uphill, south, over the rocky ridge above it – a short cut that rejoins the road at higher level. Here the road makes a wide loop around the head of a valley descending to the north-west.

The mule track is routed up the steep and rounded hillside now towering above the road, south, but you cannot see it from here. To reach it, first get onto the ridge, left, east above the road: at the end of the road-loop, a footpath 1,180m (3,871ft) – red dot on rock – leaves the road 110° SE for the top of the ridge: 20 minutes.

Continue south along the ridge top (views) and up splintered footpaths through heathland for 20 minutes to a level area with an old *mitato*. The next spring is its water supply, 20 minutes up the trail. Look west to find the best ascending footpath – there are several in the undergrowth. Once on the path, you are at last launched on the old mule track to Anopolis, via Kolokithas, Livada and Katsiveli.

After 15 minutes the path levels out, contouring around the hillside to a large well-preserved stone corbelled hut and sheepfold. An animal trough on the path just beyond marks Selya, the third spring. Few springs of the White Mountains emerge over such a tremendous view of the foothills and coast below and, as hut locations go, this must be one of the very best – a great place to camp if the timing of about 3 hours 45 minutes from Theriso and settled weather allows – for the priority is route-finding in good visibility.

A junction of footpaths develops beyond the spring. Straight on is new – a traverse and descent to the shepherds' road now far below, whilst left, heading steadily uphill, is the correct route. After 20 minutes, turn into a re-entrant (a north-west descending valley) and climb to the saddle on the skyline, 1,580m (5,184ft), reached in 30 minutes, thus completing most of the height-gain on the ascent to Kolokithas. The wild, barren mountains of the Kaloros region north-east of Melindaou are now in full view to the south-west across the valley.

147

Lose height a little to pick up the traverse to the next spur and old *mitato* (disused). From here continue across the next wide re-entrant. The fourth and last spring-served trough, at Kapsekas, is on the far side of this, a little lower down. The north/south watershed is now imminent, so fully replenish your water supply here. Ascend the next spur known as Tria Matia (Three Eyes) partly on a straight section through rocks and then continue south to the rim of the Kolokithas valley, 1,800m (5,851ft).

The south-west side of this remote valley, once worked by shepherds from Anopolis, comprises an outcrop of 'badlands', formations of forbidding appearance. On the right, to the west, a structurally unsound half-ruined *mitato* (with an unusually large interior) clings to the hillside below the rim. Note the flat floor of the valley and a central hill.

For Kolokithas *mitato* (disused) and sheepfold, either contour round or descend to cross the valley floor and then climb the central hill.

Corbelling construction cannot sustain large openings and the entrance to the main hut is typical of this. As you enter and leave you will hit your head if you forget to take it slowly. The half-built, new hut alongside was not completed before the younger shepherds abandoned this workstation, which was 10 hours by mule from Anopolis. The shepherd of Kolokithas, having sixty years experience in the Lefka Ori, has supplied some place names mentioned on these routes, which may be useful to trekkers.

The cistern is below the *mitato* (after 50 metres on the footpath south-east from the complex, drop down left, north-east). This long central hill divides the valley, forming a bridge across it to a gap in the south-east rim from where the trail continues south-east to Livada. Ay. Pnevma (2,244m/7,362ft) shows in the distance beyond Livada.

The Livada valley is about 3 kilometres in total length, orientated south-west to north-east, and 100 metres lower in altitude than the trail from Kolokithas that comes in one third of the way along it. Just before the descent, pass Pirgos *mitato* (still used) perched on the rim (shepherds may leave a guard dog). A footpath from this descends to the cistern in a rocky hollow on the valley floor. Alternatively, the mule track that now continues straight on to Katsiveli (Trek 4) turns south-west, bypassing this water supply.

Trek 1a. Livada to Theriso

This is Trek 1 in reverse.

Grade:	D
Starting point:	Livada cistern (1,800m/5,905ft)
Access:	Treks 2, 3, 4a
Finishing point:	Theriso (600m/1,968ft)
Access:	Taxi from Chania
Height loss	from Livada rim: 1,300m (4,265ft)
Approximate distance:	16km (10mls)
Time allowance:	Livada to Kolokithas *mitato*: 1hr 30mins; to Kapsekas spring: 1hr 30mins; to Selya spring: 1hr 50mins; to shepherds' road (1,100m/3,608ft): 50mins; to Theriso: 2 hrs. Total: 7hrs 40mins.

Directions

Starting from Katsiveli, see Trek 4a. Otherwise, starting from Livada cistern, leave the north side of the hollow on the footpath that bears left, uphill, to Pirgos *mitato*. From the *mitato* the mule track heads north-west for Kolokithas valley rim (2 kilometres, 1 hour), where it bears right, losing height to continue north-west along the central hill to the *mitato*. From there, reverse Trek 1, picking up the trail north via the ruined *mitato* on the west rim.

Trek 2. Kambi to Livada via Volikas Refuge

Grade:	D
Starting point:	Kambi (600m/1,968ft)
Access:	KTEL Kambi bus or taxi from Chania
Finishing point:	Livada cistern (1,800m/5,905ft)
Access:	ongoing Treks 1a, 3a, 4
Height gain:	1,300m (4,265ft)
Approximate distance:	12km (7.5mls)
Time allowance:	Kambi to Volikas Refuge (1,480m/4,855ft): 3hrs 30mins; Volikas to Spathi pass

(1,900m/6,233ft): 2hrs 45mins; pass to Stavrou Seli (1,900m/6,233ft): 2 hrs; to Livada cistern (1,800m/6,854ft): 1 hr. Total: 9hrs 15mins.

Volikas EOZ Mountain Refuge (1,480m/4,855ft) is sited under a long crag with a spring, on the north/south footpath between Kambi and Livada (not a mule track), now a branch of the E4 Trail. Spathi (2,045m/6,709ft) is the peak commonly climbed from this footpath. However, beyond Spathi the route continues south less easily, having to cross a valley of confusing ridges and hollows (chains of limestone sink-holes) to reach the north-eastern rim of Livada. Although the ascent of Spathi is due south from Volikas over relatively easy terrain, a crossing of the 'badlands' valley of sink-holes (named 'Gourgoutha tou Spathiou') would be very difficult in poor visibility even for those who are familiar with it (no E4 Trail poles in 1998). Even if the weather seems settled you must be equipped to camp anywhere if mist develops and be prepared to re-trace your steps if it persists. Mist with drizzle and rain sometimes lasts for three days. Alternatively, ordinary afternoon mist may clear by the evening in a pattern that lasts for a few days at a time. In settled conditions, this is a scenically superb route in a very rugged part of the mountains still almost free of access roads. Volikas EOZ Refuge is locked (book in advance with the EOZ), but its terrace makes a pleasant camp-spot on the total ascent of 1,300m (4,226ft) to the rim of the Livada valley.

This trek suits from early May if snow on the northern slopes lies in streaks, but on-going routes from Livada may be limited to Treks 1a, 4, 8a and 6a. Take food for two and a half or three days.

Directions

Follow Walk 15 to Volikas Refuge. Take on water here for the ascent to Livada, for unless there is snow to melt, the next water source is the Livada valley cistern.

From Volikas, climb up through the crags (E4 Trail pole) above and a little to the left of the refuge. Ascend due south to the top of the spur. Beyond, the path continues up beside a minor watercourse draining from a small amphitheatre-shaped

Pausing on the north rim of Livada, Stavrou Seli (May)

valley. Turn right in this valley and ascend through rocks to the west rim. An old stone corbelled hut at the end of this ridge is the last man-made shelter on the route. Looking west, the mountainside now comprises a mass of black ridges, hollows and crags.

Continue south up the ridge on easy gravel to a level area divided by a shallow furrow running north-west. A rocky conical peak rises beyond. Bear left across the meadow to find the easiest route to the summit. The view from the top suits those who do not want to do the full climb to Spathi – the higher peak now just along the ridge. Spathi's north face is a sheer cliff above a deep circular valley. (The chapel seen far below belongs to Kares.) Some footpath maps show the path crossing the cliff, but it goes, of course, to the pass, right, south-west of the peak.

Now descend to the small saddle below and head straight for this pass, gradually gaining height: 40 minutes. *For Spathi summit:* turn up left and then descend to the pass from the summit. The pass overlooks the 'badlands' valley, with Ay. Pnevma (2,254m/ 7,395ft) on the far side. The rim of Livada is not in sight from this position as it is around the corner to the right, below Ay. Pnevma: about 1.7 kilometres in direct distance.

151

Select a route across these various hollows and rocky ridges in the general direction of 160° SE, starting off by bearing right over a large rock below the pass. If snow is still thawing in the hollows take extra care at the weak edges of these drifts. Cross this area with patience. As you cannot always see your way, it is quite normal to arrive at a dead-end crag: in this situation, just try another option.

Near the rim of Livada the terrain gets back to normal: easy gravel underfoot. This is the Stavrou Seli 'cross pass' between Ay. Pnevma or Ornio (2,153m/7,063ft). The steep and unattractive 100 metre descent to the valley floor is not clearly defined – choose your route. The cistern is about 1.5 kilometres (0.9 miles) down the valley to the south-west in a rocky hollow just below Pirgos *mitato* (still used), which appears as an apparent pile of rocks on the south-west rim. Similarly, Livada *mitato* (disused, provides shelter) blends into the hillside opposite Pirgos: this, too, is just above the water source.

Keep straight down the centre of the valley heading south-west on a well-defined footpath that crosses various rocky hollows. In spring the cistern may be buried under a snowdrift, in which case you would melt snow for water – or continue on to Katsiveli (Trek 4a) where the cistern will have snow-melt (boil it).

Trek 2a. Livada to Kambi

This is Trek 2 in reverse. See Trek 4a.

Grade:	D
Starting point:	Livada cistern (1,800m/5,904ft)
Access:	Treks 1, 3 and 4a
Finishing point:	Kambi (600m/1,968ft)
Access:	KTEL Kambi bus or taxi from Chania
Height gain:	to Livada rim, 100m (3,28ft)
Height loss:	1,300m (4,265ft)
Approximate distance:	12km (7.5mls)
Time allowance:	Livada cistern to Stavrou Seli pass: 1hr 15mins; to Spathi pass: 2hrs; to Volikas Refuge: 2 hrs, to Kambi: 2 hrs. Total: 7hrs 15mins.

Northern mountainsides are steep and extremely rugged in places: good visibility is needed for this descent. Apart from the correct footpath, the only escape route is the Madaro shepherds' road (a long tramp) that terminates (1998) below the ridge, 1 kilometre east of Volikas Refuge.

Trek 3. Askyfou via Niato and Grias Soros to Livada (E4 Trail)

Grade:	E
Starting point:	Ammoudari, Askyfou (790m/2,591ft)
Access:	KTEL Sfakia bus or taxi from Vrises or Hora Sfakion
Finishing point:	Livada cistern (1,800m/5,905ft)
Access:	ongoing Treks 1a, 2a, 4
Height gain:	1,310m (4,297ft)
Height loss:	300m/984ft
Height of Grias Soros:	2,331m (7,647ft)
Approximate distance:	16km (10mls)
Time allowance:	Askyfou to E4 Trail trailhead (1,300m/4,264ft): 2hrs 15mins; to last cistern: 10mins; to pass (1,700m/5,577ft): 3hrs 30mins; to the unnamed saddle (2,000m/6,561ft): 2 hrs; to Grias Soros saddle (2,100m/6,889ft): 50mins; Grias Soros saddle to Livada cistern (1,800m/5,774ft): 1hr 30mins. Total: 10hr 15mins. Optional round detour to Grias Soros summit: 1hr 45mins. Note: timings for E4 Trail variation over Kastro probably similar.

This is Crete's top hillwalking challenge. British Army cadets use it for (voluntary) training purposes. Build up skills and experience on other Lefka Ori routes before you tackle it so that you are familiar with what to expect, what you need and your likely rate of walking. In common with some other of the treks, it is not an expedition for those who have to rush back to the airport as bad weather might delay progress. Although now designated a branch of the E4 Trail, this is another of the very old routes across the range – just a route, not a mule track.

The main problem is the traverse of the north flank of Kastro, a 2.5 hours struggle across a steep scree-lined slope, eroded and loose, to reach an essential pass at 1,700m (5,577ft). The EOZ have waymarked the E4 Trail on an alternative route that bypasses part of the old loose-surfaced traverse. This climbs the south side of Kastro's north ridge, to pass over the spine of it at an altitude above the level of the pass. Waymarking (1998) ends here: installation of the poles is very difficult for amateurs on foot in such a remote place.

The summit view from Grias Soros showing the essential pass beside the north flank of Mt. Kastro

The approach from Livada in the west is not much easier (although food supplies will now weigh less) as there is no escaping the Kastro traverse, by which time there may be no alternative but to hurry on, because your water supply is low. If the scree slope is very bad it is possible to descend to the valley below and work through the rocks here. An initial escape option is more available to those who start from Niato and it could be useful to tackle the main effort first, even though you have more to carry. Either way, from Livada or Niato, stages, food and water supply need careful planning.

154

Note that, whilst some maps mark the E4 Trail route where it is, others mark it as being on the traditional route: in conjunction with these notes – read the map contours. Do not set off in unsettled weather as you need good visibility the whole way and, once you are on the trail, take note of your position at all times. If a mist develops, stay in place, on low rations (food-digesting needs water) so that you can then move safely on, or back, when conditions allow. Take a water bottle on any detours. Remember nights are colder at higher altitude and for a good night's sleep you need to be suitably warm. Take food supplies for three days and a minimum of six litres of water per person: two litres on the trail, three litres for the overnight camp and one spare litre for the morning.

Although melted snow provides drinking water, unless you are equipped for snow mountaineering, steep drifts that linger through June could block your passage. As a rule the best time of year for this venture is mid-September to mid-October – after the heat of summer and in between the unsettled periods that are normal to the Summer to Autumn seasonal change.

Directions

In the afternoon, follow Walk 27 to Niato, (where the E4 Trail signpost notes 'Livada 6.5 hours') and then continue on to the start of the E4 Trail trailhead beyond the north-west pass. Note the water supply options mentioned in Walk 27 and camp nearby for an early morning start.

In the evening check out the route options: follow Walk 27 down the valley from the Niato north-west pass to the second old barrel-vaulted cistern under the lone prickly oak tree. The huge grey slab of Kastro's north flank now looms above, although you cannot see around the corner to the 'essential' pass from here. The traditional route starts from a short distance up the gully behind this cistern. It bears right, up through rocks to get onto the hillside where there are sparse trees. Beyond, and out of sight of the cistern, it crosses beneath a big open dip in the mountainside before gaining more height for the traverse proper. From there the pass is in sight, so then it is a matter of working towards it. The valley below this traverse comprises passable, but tortuous, rock formations, which is why this old route crossed the scree slope above it.

Alternatively, consider the E4 Trail waymarked up to the south side of the north-flank ridge. (EOZ committee members recommend a guide as the going is 'very bad'.) Rocky terrain (strenuous) is a feature of the initial ascent and loose rocks make descents (with backpack) very trying. Set your mind to tackling whichever route you choose with patience and care, for as you can see, there is no room for errors on these remote mountainsides.

The essential pass, once it is reached, is the entrance to a high valley of much more hospitable appearance, rather like Roussies on the way to Katsiveli. Here there are various faint footpath-options made by shepherds, hunters, walkers, and quartz collectors.

The next objective is the saddle on the north side of an unnamed conical peak (2,213m/7,260ft) just east of Grias Soros. From the west end of the valley, make your way up to about 2,000m (6,561ft), under the ridge, which is the northern rim of the 'badlands' depression now in view to the south-west. This is the Pavlia Harlara ('Pav-lee-AH HAR-larra') a 6 square kilometre moonscape of black, white, grey and red rock formations, slabs and hollows. Minor rock scrambling ability is needed for crossings of this grim-looking region. The nearest access road serves the Ammoutsera valley under Kakovoli (see Trek 8).

From the saddle north of, under, the unnamed conical peak, the next objective is the pass (2,100m/6,889ft) north side of the next conical peak, which is Grias Soros (2,331m/7,647ft). Ay. Pnevma (Mount of the Holy Spirit) with its ruined summit chapel and south-east facing crags is 310° NW. Weather permitting this pass is a good place to camp for an evening summit ascent – take daysack essentials on this detour.

Ascent of Grias Soros (2,331m/7,650ft), second highest peak in the Lefka Ori. In places, veins of solid rock punctuate a thin layer of eroded scree as the gradient gets steeper, providing welcome hand and footholds for the climb. The summit area of this huge cone is small, so that you feel even more like an ant in a vast landscape. The busy north coast road is in sight far below, but southwards the panorama from Kastro to Pachnes is without doubt the most extraordinary in all Crete. The 'sinister' Pavlia

Harlara is such a deterrent to development that not a single man-made object is in sight. It looks its weird best just before sunset when lengthening shadows define west-facing hillsides and hues of yellow and orange replace the stark midday glare on the scree slopes. After dark, the lights of the north coast twinkle far below, but no light or unnatural sound disturbs the Pavlia Harlara.

For Livada: from the Grias Soros pass take a compass bearing 300° NW (down the valley under Ay. Pnevma) to part of the Livada valley, which is now in sight beyond it. In advance, assess the best route down to and along the valley, where low rocky ridges separate sandy, flat plains. At the north-west end a footpath beside a huge rock funnel (sink-hole) of the type that holds thawing snow for many months, gains height to the rim where a small stone wind-shelter and an E4 Trail pole heralds your arrival at Livada.

The shepherds' footpath heads downhill straight for the cistern in a flat-floored hollow on the valley floor, and halfway down, E4 Trail poles direct you left, past Livada *mitato* (disused, provides shelter) that looks like a pile of rocks. This route bypasses the cistern and is therefore a marginally quicker way west to Katsiveli (Trek 4).

Trek 3a. Livada to Niato and Askyfou (E4 Trail)

Grade:	E
Starting point:	Livada cistern (1,800m/5,905ft)
Access:	Treks 4a and 1, 2
Finishing point:	Ammoudari, Askyfou (790m/2,591ft
Access:	KTEL Sfakia bus, or taxi from Vrises or Hora Sfakion
Height gain:	300m (984ft)
Height loss:	1,310m (4,297ft)
Approximate distance:	16km (10mls)
Time allowance:	Livada cistern to Grias Soros saddle (2,100m/6,889ft): 2hrs 10mins; to unnamed saddle (2,000m/6,416ft): 40mins; to pass (1,700m/5,577ft): 1hr 30mins; to 'last' cistern: 3hrs 30mins; to Ammoudari: 1hr 30mins. Total: 9hrs 20mins.

See Trek 3. From Livada, take food supplies for two and a half days and minimum of six litres of water per person: two litres on the trail, three litres for the overnight camp and one litre for the morning.

Directions

Starting from Livada cistern, leave the hollow, east, on a footpath up to the pass on the south-east rim where there is a small stone wind-shelter and the last E4 Trail pole (1998). The pass overlooks a remote valley under Ay. Pnevma with the conical Grias Soros in the distance. On a bearing 120° SE, note a dip, or pass, on the skyline north of Grias Soros – this is your first objective. The footpath along the valley directs you to the best route through rocks and up to this spot. From there reverse Trek 3.

Trek 4. Livada to Katsiveli (E4 Trail)

Grade:	C/D
Starting point:	Livada cistern (1,800m/5,905ft)
Access:	Treks 1, 2, 3
Finishing point:	Katsiveli cistern (1,940m/6,364ft)
Access:	ongoing Treks 5, 8a, 9b
Height gain:	180m (590ft)
Height loss:	40m (131ft)
Approximate distance:	3km (1.8mls)
Time allowance:	1hr 25mins.

This is a well-tramped mule track between the two valleys.

Directions

Leave Livada on the central footpath up to the south-west rim (E4 Trail pole). Turn sharp left and head south, traversing above a valley. As the path ascends a ridge, note an E4 Trail signpost on the left, above the path: 'Livada 1 hour, Niato 7.5 hours, Askyfou 9.5 hours.' The EOZ refuge (locked) appears on the skyline. The refuge overlooks Katsiveli and the path down, 5 minutes, continues just to the right of it.

En route from Livada you pass the EOZ refuge, just before Katsiveli

Trek 4a. Katsiveli to Livada (E4 Trail)

This is Trek 4 in reverse.

Grade:	C/D
Time allowance:	1hr 10mins.

The Katsiveli valley, a natural junction on the main south/north mule track between Anopolis and Theriso, has been important to shepherds since the Iron Age. The new road from Anopolis, terminating just below Roussies (1998), lately enables the shepherds (unburdened with backpacks) to reach Katsiveli from this parking place after only 1 hour's walking. The road will eventually reach the valley, ensuring its status (in Anopolis) as a viable workstation, and minor improvements are already underway.

Katsiveli's sheep troughs and large concrete cistern are fed by snow-melt and a *lastico* (black pipe) from a high-level spring (not running by Autumn). E4 Trail poles form a trestle on the *mitato* terrace. (Some people may think this is a better use for them.) A round stone 'Koumi' hut on top of the rocky knoll adjacent is intended as a shelter for passers-by (new

159

The Katsiveli mitato (bothy)

project 1998). The accumulated litter might go when the road arrives.

Katsiveli is also an important stage on the E4 Trail from Omalos/Kallergi. In 1992 the EOZ opened a stone-built refuge on the northern rim of the valley. (This is locked. Book with the EOZ.)

Shepherds will be busy in and around the Katsiveli area from June to October, or even November, depending on water supply and work projects.

Directions

Via the footpath through the cutting between the 'Koumi' knoll and the *mitato*, ascend to the EOZ refuge on the north rim. On the path up, two names and the year '1992, Geneva, Syria' are tooled into a rock in Arabic. More tooling over the refuge door lintel suggests these two vandals must have been waiting for thick mist to clear. The mule track continues north steeply downhill from the refuge (E4 Trail signpost above the path on the way down). Another E4 Trail pole marks the south-west rim of Livada. From here the Livada's two *mitatos* are in sight, one third of the way down the valley: both are of the old style, looking like piles of rocks. Pirgos (still used) is on the skyline to the left, on a spur, north-west, and Livada (disused) is opposite it on the other side. The cistern is in a rocky hollow on the valley floor, directly below the *mitatos*. A central footpath leads 3 kilometres (1.8 miles) straight down Livada to the north-east rim (for Kambi, Trek 2a) and otherwise, the trail to Kolokithas (Trek 1a) leaves from beside Pirgos *mitato* and the E4 Trail via Grias Soros to Askyfou, leaves from behind Livada *mitato* (Trek 3a).

Trek 5. Katsiveli to Potamos (E4 Trail)

Grade:	C/D
Starting point:	Katsiveli cistern (1,940m/6,364ft)
Access:	Treks 4 and 8
Finishing point:	Potamos valley north (1,750m/5,741ft)
Access:	ongoing Treks 6a and 7
Height gain:	40m (131ft)
Height loss:	150m (492ft)
Approximate distance:	2km (1.2mls)
Time allowance:	1hr.

Now part of the E4 Trail to Omalos and Kallergi, this is also a well-used shepherds' mule track and easy to follow. No doubt it is due to be replaced by a road from Katsiveli as there is good grazing at Potamos.

Directions

From Katsiveli cistern, turn west alongside a wall on the path to the low west rim of the valley. After 45 minutes arrive to overlook the Potamos valley. Klissida, a ruined *mitato* complex, is below the path to the left. Petrathe *mitato* (still used) is seen on top of a hill across the valley to the west. Descend to an open cistern (poor water) directly below, in a mass of thorny burnet.

For Melindaou/Kallergi (E4 Trail) – Trek 6a – reverse the route notes of Trek 6: leave the valley heading north-west on a footpath up the west side of a gully. *For Trek 7:* turn south on footpaths down the Potamos valley. *For a rare view of the Samaria Gorge:* (no through route) detour west to the end of the smaller valley below Petrathe *mitato*.

The Potamos valley

Potamos is the northern extension of the Eligas Gorge. Some maps show a footpath down the gorge to the south coast, but this is wrong. At the top a 'waterfall' cliff face and adjacent crags block the route to walkers or climbers without equipment (see Walk 47).

Potamos, worked by shepherds from Ay. Ioannis and Anopolis, is the valley seen to the south-east from the summit of Melindaou – it lies between Pachnes and the east rim of the Samaria Gorge. Alternatively, if you arrive from Katsiveli in the east, you will not see much of it in advance. There are four cisterns and *mitatos* in the valley. At the top of the valley's northern extension, just off the E4 Trail, is Pirou. Opposite the mule track from Katsiveli, on a hilltop to the west, is Petrathe ('Petra-theh'). Down the middle of the valley, on the west side, is Koumi ('Koo-mee') and, lastly, as the Eligas Gorge develops, there is Potamos. All these *mitatos* could provide shelter in bad weather, although from June to October they may be in use, or half-use.

Trek 5a. Potamos to Katsiveli

This is Trek 5 in reverse.

Grade:	C/D
Starting point:	Potamos valley north (1,750m/5,741ft)
Access:	Ongoing Treks 6a and 7
Finishing point:	Katsiveli cistern (1,940m/6,364ft)
Access:	Treks 4 and 8
Height gain:	150m (492ft)
Height loss:	40m (131ft)
Approximate distance:	2km (1.2mls)
Time allowance:	1hr 20mins.

Trek 6. Omalos/Kallergi to Potamos and Katsiveli via Melendaou (E4 Trail)

Grade:	D
Starting point:	Kallergi Refuge (1,680m/5,511ft)
Access:	Walk 4 from Xyloscala

Finishing point:	Potamos valley north (1,750m/5,741ft)
Access:	Ongoing Treks 5a and 7
Height gain:	500m (1,640ft)
Height loss:	350m (1,148ft)
Approximate distance:	10km (6mls)
Time allowance:	Kallergi to E4 turn-off (1,600m/5,249ft) for Melendaou: 1hr 15mins; to summit area (2,100m/7,996ft): 2 hrs 45mins; to Potamos valley: 1hr 30mins. Total: 5hrs 30mins.

This waymarked branch of the E4 Trail to Katsiveli via the summit of Melindaou (2,133m/8,122ft) is the first stage of a two-day route (during long daylight hours) from Omalos to Anopolis. From Katsiveli (Trek 8a) a mule track continues south, meeting the Anopolis shepherds' road just below Roussies (1998).

Although unavoidably downgraded by the new road, this very scenic route takes in almost all the elements that characterise the Madares and the heart of the White Mountains.

The Potamos valley in late May

163

Take food for two days. Water at Potamos needs boiling. Katsiveli has good water until September. If west-facing mountainsides are free of snow, this route suits from May to November. Note: Potamos and Katsiveli offer other route choices, but these extend the trek to two and a half days minimum: consider this in advance of setting off.

Directions

From Xyloscala follow Walks 4 and 5 to Poria, beyond Kallergi Refuge. For the E4 Trail continue about 800m along the shepherds' road to where E4 Trail poles waymark the ascent (see Walk 5).

Following a shepherds' workaday route, the E4 Trail bypasses the summit by a short distance and continues east above Melindaou's great stratified cliff. It then turns away from the gorge, crossing rocky outcrops on a steady descent to a flat-floored valley where there is an open cistern (poor water) that is dry by Autumn.

Leave this valley heading east, marked by an E4 Trail pole and a small stone wind-shelter. Then either turn sharp left for Pirou *mitato* (shelter), or bear right, to the south-east, down across this next valley (open cistern) to a small pass that is the entrance to the Potamos valley proper. Descend to an open cistern (poor water) in a mass of thorny burnet.

For Katsiveli (Trek 5a): ascend to the east, directly above this cistern, to pick up the mule track to Katsiveli. It passes just above a ruined *mitato* complex. Reverse the route notes of Trek 5.

Trek 6a. Potamos to Kallergi Refuge

This is Trek 6 in reverse.

Grade:	D
Starting point:	Potamos valley north (1,790m/5,872ft)
Access:	Treks 5 and 7a
Finishing point:	Kallergi Refuge (1,680m/5,511ft)
Access:	Walk 4 to Xyloscala, or shepherds' road to Omalos Plateau
Height gain:	310m (1,017ft)
Height loss:	500m (1,640ft)
Approximate distance:	10km (6mls)

Time allowance:	Potamos to Melendaou summit area: 3hrs 30mins; to Kallergi Refuge: 2hrs 30mins. Total: 6hrs.

Trek 7. Potamos to Ay. Ioannis via Zaranokefala

Grade:	D
Starting point:	Potamos valley north (1,790m/5,872ft)
Access:	Trek 6 and 5
Finishing point:	Ay. Ioannis (800m/2,624ft)
Access:	taxi from Hora Sfakion, or ongoing walks
Height gain:	300m (984ft)
Height loss:	1,100m (3,608ft)
Approximate distance:	11km (7mls)
Time allowance:	Potamos valley north to Potamos *mitato* (1,600m/5,249ft): 40mins; ascent to Zaranokefala spring (1,900m/6,233ft): 3hrs 15mins; descent to Kroussia (1,240m/4,068ft): 2hrs 20mins; to Ay. Ioannis: 1hr 15mins. Total: 7hrs 30mins.

Contouring along a shelf in the south-west facing summit crag of Zaranokefala, high above the Eligas Gorge, this ancient droving trail between Anopolis (or Ay. Ioannis) and the Omalos Plateau is the most dramatic of all the mule tracks, affording stupendous views down to the south coast. A small but permanent spring is the all-important treasure of the crag. Once you know where to look, the line of the shelf can be seen from the boats that ply the south coast, or from the summit of Gingilos (Walk 3).

However, there is a problem – after climbing out of the Potamos valley, the path contours into a deep re-entrant above a long steep drop, and sheltered from the sun, a last snowdrift can block the trail here well into June. Reserve this trek for the period between July and November and also avoid it in a strong wind as some sections are rather exposed.

Directions

Halfway down the Potamos valley, 300m south of Koumi *mitato*, take on water at a barrel-vaulted cistern: allow two litres for the long ascent. The ascent starts from Potamos *mitato*, another 20 minutes down the valley. Pass the remains (on the east side) of an Argentinean aeroplane that crashed in 1957. (Throughout the mountains, almost every *mitato* has some useful piece of its aluminium fuselage.)

Avoid the path from the aeroplane as it is loose and rather exposed at high level even though it does join the main trail. Instead, continue down to Potamos *mitato* on the west side of the dry river bed. Note the rare ambelitsa tree, endemic to the Omalos region, in front of the *mitato,* from which the traditional *katsouna* – shepherds' crook of Sfakia – is made.

The ascent to the crag takes more than 3 hours, which is why, on a hot day, you need lots of water. Potamos cistern is another 100 metres down the river bed, on the right-hand side.

Take the path up the opposite bank to reach the main trail that zigzags up the scree slope of a steep shallow re-entrant. After this initial ascent, and now high above the Eligas Gorge, contour around a rocky spur into the deep re-entrant that retains the snowdrift in the spring. Beyond it, the path climbs to a long shelf. This is a grim-looking place – an outcrop of 'badlands' rock high above an awesome drop into the gorge. A dancing heat haze can enhance its inhospitable appearance.

The next objective is a distinct saddle on a spur at higher level, in the middle distance. Continue along the shelf almost to where it ends in an outcrop of ugly black rock (called 'Mavra Harlara'). Unless high winds have dispersed them, cairns mark the best route across this. With the saddle as your known goal, make your way up, gaining height steadily on this traverse. The Zaranokefala crag looms above and beyond the saddle.

On the saddle, face east into the mountain. Up in the crag, a brown (or green) horizontal line of thorny burnet marks the contouring shelf. Directly in front of you, a vein of vertical rock guides you up the continuation of the route. After about 200 metres, turn off to the right and cross to the next descending spur. Beyond it the mule track is easier to see as it zigzags up the steep hillside to reach the crag. Just before the crag, note a very steep and unfrequented rocky footpath up beside it. This is one way of getting to the Pachnes summit area. Avoid this in unsettled conditions as this level at 2,200m (7,218ft), although easy underfoot, is confusingly featureless in poor visibility. Under some circumstances this could be an escape route to Roussies (Trek 8 and 8a). However, about 1 kilometre from this point you leave the crag for the top of a spur. Anopolis is in view from there and you will be visible on the skyline (through binoculars) to villagers far below.

About 5 minutes along the shelf, pass a walled-in overhang. There are more overhangs beside the spring further on, but this is the only real shelter in the crag. Be very careful not to contaminate the spring as you get drinking water by removing protective stones – use your cooking pan as a baler. If you camp here, and defecate, do this onto a stone and throw this (not the toilet paper – burn that or carry it out) carefully down the steep cliff, because, despite its eagles'-eyrie feel, this is a mule track still in regular use. Also, in this apparently remote spot, during the hunting season (September onwards) do not be alarmed if parties of hunters pass in the night. Cretans like walking after dark, because it is cooler. Shepherds accustomed to the terrain can even run at night on some of these rocky trails.

Heading up to the Zaranokefala crag with the saddle in the foreground

Take on two litres of water for the long descent to Ay. Ioannis. Continue along the shelf to the south-west facing corner of the crag, where layered flat rocks make good seats as you pause to look at the view of the coast far below. Half of Ay. Roumeli beach is in sight and so are the two Turkish forts high above the west side of the Eligas Gorge.

Now enhanced by the welcome reappearance of mountain cypresses, the path turns east under the crag's south face, heading for the level top of a spur. From there, Anopolis is in view to the south-east. Turn south for 200 metres along the spur and then head east steeply down a main footpath in amongst several goat paths. Still very far down, the rooftops of Ay. Ioannis appear below pine forested slopes.

Cross a shallow gully and enter sparse pine forest, keeping straight on south-eastwards down the mule track to Kroussia, a large clearing where there are three open cisterns (poor water). A shepherds' road from Ay. Ioannis comes in from the south. Follow this for 200 metres to Vitsiles ('Vit-see-lezz') *mitato* (shelter). From here it is a long tramp to Ay. Ioannis. The old mule track down a forested ravine is quicker, although as usual it is broken up and stony underfoot. 4 kilometres of asphalt road links Ay. Ioannis with Anopolis via Aradena. To avoid it, you might consider the Anopolis shepherds' path that bypasses Ay. Ioannis on a direct, but tougher, and nowadays very unfrequented, route down to the Aradena Gorge.

For Anopolis: (see Walk 42) leave Kroussia heading east on a footpath heading down (bear left) through the forest, for 4 kilometres, to the west rim of the Aradena Gorge (640m): your 'aiming-off' destination, for there are many sheep paths in the forest. The shepherds' gorge-crossing is difficult to find from this side – instead, turn south and make your way along through the forest within sight of the gorge rim, to Aradena.

For Ay. Ioannis: leave Kroussia on the road, peeling off it after a couple of minutes to the left, south, on a stony mule track. Gain a little height before starting the descent of the ravine. Pass a walled, disused orchard on the right. Just when you think you must have missed the village altogether, a *kalderimi* leaves the east side of the ravine, heading for a big concrete water tank. Walk down the road and bear left. What was a 1930s-style schoolhouse is now the *kafeneon* – it is the last building of the village; or the first if you had arrived from Aradena. From the *kafeneon* either descend to Sellouda for Ay. Roumeli (Walks 38 and 39) or tramp the road to Anopolis: 1 hour 40 minutes walking, via the bridge over the Aradena Gorge.

Trek 7a. Ay. Ioannis to Potamos via Zaranokefala

This is Trek 7 in reverse.

Grade:	D
Starting point:	Ay. Ioannis (800m/3,046ft)
Access:	Taxi from Hora Sfakion
Finishing point:	Potamos valley north (1,790m/5,872ft)
Access:	Ongoing Treks 5a and 6a
Height gain:	1,100m (3,608ft)
Height loss:	300m (984ft)
Approximate distance:	11km (7mls)
Time allowance:	Ay. Ioannis to Kroussia (1,240m/4,068ft): 2hrs 20mins; to Zaranokefala spring (1,900m/6,233ft): 3hrs 20mins; spring to Potamos *mitato* (1,600m/5,249ft)): 2hrs 30mins; to Potamos valley north – E4 Trail (1,740m/5,708ft): 1 hr. Total: 9hrs 10mins.

The long steep ascent above Ay. Ioannis makes this a more strenuous way of doing it, but an approach from the south may suit your itinerary. Take food for two and a half to three days and two litres of water for the ascent-effort to be supplemented by a brew up at Kroussia if necessary. Take on supplies at Hora Sfakion or Anopolis and arrange a lift or a taxi to Ay. Ioannis.

Directions
Walk up to the concrete village water tank and, just beyond it, bear right, going west, onto a stony footpath heading for the steep, forested ravine above the village. From Kroussia cisterns, the mule track continues the ascent north-westwards (see Trek 7).

Trek 8. Anopolis to Katsiveli

Grade:	D
Starting point:	Anopolis (600m/1,968ft)
Access:	KTEL Sfakia–Anopolis bus or taxi from Chania
Finishing point:	Katsiveli cistern (1,940m/6,364ft)
Access:	Ongoing Treks 4a and 5
Height gain:	1,450m (4,757ft)
Height loss:	110m (360ft)
Approximate distance:	17km (10.5mls)
Time allowance:	Anopolis to Vigla cistern (1,300m/4,265ft): 3hrs 30mins; to Roussies pass (2,050m/7,806ft): 4hrs 15mins; to Katsiveli: 1hr 25mins. Total: 9hrs 10mins.

Entering the Ammoutsera valley with hut and cistern just below

This route, a mule track, is on all maps. Part of it may be shown as a footpath, and part of it as a road (the road is under construction, new sections being built year by year). It is the easiest approach to Pachnes and other parts of the Madares,

especially now that the new road terminates just below Roussies (1998), the customary base camp for the ascent of Pachnes. From Anopolis it may be possible to arrange a lift to this road head (enquire) – the road surface is very rough. Purists will want to use what is left of the old mule track where possible and, initially, this is routed up the steep forested ravine almost due north of Anopolis *plateia*.

Take food supplies for two or three days according to your ongoing route plan and two litres of water for the initial ascent to be supplemented by a brew up at Vigla if necessary. This trek is suitable from May until the first snow of winter.

Directions

Leave Anopolis *plateia* on the west side. Turn north at the next junction, at Kostas' taverna, on a road heading straight for the mountains. After 12 minutes the road forks: bear left for 1 minute, as far as a large animal shed on the right. Bear right onto a track from the shed, and then continue north, heading straight for a ravine on a footpath through the pine forest. Keep on the footpath as it crosses a road.

This shepherds' road to Ammoutsera and beyond (where you are going) turns east at the foot of the ravine, on the start of its long, winding but very scenic climb. As ever, the mule track takes the direct route, zigzagging up the ravine. After the ravine opens out (for at least the second time) Vigla cistern appears at last – a huge barrel-vaulted creation entirely in keeping with this very old trail. The shepherds' road is seen traversing the steep hill above and a slip road from it, heading east, connects down to Vigla. 'Vigle' was the name for village look-out stations – this one is at the head of the adjacent east spur; a small footpath to it leads up from the ravine bed some distance downhill from the cistern.

The mule track continues west from the cistern, gaining height before zigzagging up the highest part of the ravine. The hillside finally levels out beyond the last cypress trees at 1,600m (5249ft).

Rejoin the shepherds' road as it enters a long valley – the true entrance to the high mountains. The road gains height in loops, but walkers can take the mule track short cut up the centre of the valley. Just before the pass at the top, turn up right to rejoin the road. Beyond the pass the Ammoutsera valley, a moonscape of black rocks and sandy basins, is bordered on the north-eastern side by the Kakovoli ridge.

Below the pass a small hut and a concrete cistern, once important to the old trail, are now almost redundant. Continue on the road – as the rock is black the road does not show up as an unsightly scar, seen in other areas. In the distance, Grias Soros and other peaks border the far side of the Pavlia Harlara depression, its weird rock formations partly in view as you gain height up the road.

Tramp the road to its terminus (1998) that is under a steep hill of black rock 18 kilometres from Anopolis. The great bulk of Trocharis (2,410m/7,906ft), with its fascinatingly long scree slopes, is just across the deep valley to the south-west. The ascent to Roussies ('Roo-see-ess') from here takes about 20 minutes. Roussies is a small 'hanging' valley with a stone hut, which sleeps three, and a cistern with good water. This camp spot for the ascent of Pachnes (Trek 9) is often very draughty: campers have built windbreaks. For shepherds it is a useful water point for their animals on the trail. (Note that on some maps Roussies is wrongly named 'Koumi'.) Roussies is the highest pass on the whole south/north traverse (hence the draught). An E4 Trail signpost marks the turn-off for Pachnes summit.

The mule track continues north along the valley, with easy gravel underfoot. This 1 kilometre stretch ends at another high pass where a snowdrift may block the trail until mid-June. Sheep and mules are not brought up from Anopolis until this thaws. (Before that, some older sheep make their own way up.) If the trail is blocked, climb up around the snowdrift on the east side, which is less steep.

Descend from the pass to a small rocky ridge between two valleys: the east valley is quite deep. Gingilos crag is in view to the north-west, across the Samaria Gorge. Continue above the deep valley to the next pass. The Katsiveli valley is now just below, with the EOZ refuge on its northern rim.

Trek 8a. Katsiveli to Anopolis

This is Trek 8 in reverse.

Grade:	D
Starting point:	Katsiveli cistern (1,940m/6,363ft)
Access:	Treks 4 and 5a
Finishing point:	Anopolis *plateia* (600m/1,968ft)
Access:	KTEL Sfakia–Anopolis bus, or taxi from Hora Sfakion
Height gain:	110m (360ft)
Height loss:	1,450m (4,757ft)
Approximate distance:	17km (10.5mls)
Time allowance:	Katsiveli to Roussies (2,050m/6,725ft): 1hr 40mins; Roussies to Vigla cistern (1,300m/4,265ft): 2hrs 30mins; Vigla to Anopolis: 2 hrs. Total: 6hrs 10mins.

Katsiveli is 150 metres lower than two high passes that rise to about 2,100m (6,889ft) on the route south. Scenery along the way is spectacular and varied, although the shepherds' new road, when it is reached, inevitably renders this walk disappointing to walkers. There are no E4 Trail poles, but the route is well tramped and, in reasonable visibility, not difficult to follow. In 1998 the road ended below Roussies, but when completed it is likely to replace the rest of the mule track, in which case you would just follow this road south-east from Katsiveli. Note: Roussies is wrongly named 'Koumi' on some maps.

Directions

From Katsiveli cistern turn 130° SE for the mule track that passes through rocks and zigzags up to the south-eastern rim of the valley. A long traverse south, above a deep valley, now follows, ending at a small rocky ridge that forms a division between this and another, smaller valley. Above and beyond the ridge, bear right towards a wide saddle on the skyline. From here, Roussies pass is in sight, 1 kilometre down the valley to the south-east. If a snowdrift still blocks the trail here, work round it on the eastern side.

At Roussies, where there is a small stone hut and cistern, an E4 Trail signpost marks the turn-off for the ascent of Pachnes to the south-west (Trek 9). Trocharis (2,410m/7,907ft) with its long scree slopes, dominates the view south across the deep, almost semicircular, valley beyond.

The trail now descends steeply, over black rock lower down, (keep right) to meet the shepherds' road after 15 minutes. Just beyond, a fairly long section of the mule track provides an optional short cut down to the Ammoutsera valley, now in sight below the Kakovoli ridge.

At the south end of Ammoutsera, where there is a small stone hut and cistern, continue over the pass to overlook the next valley. About 100 metres further on, red paint marks the place where you can clamber down over rocks to rejoin the mule track: a useful short cut down the centre of the valley. Rejoin the road as it heads south out of the valley. In a few minutes, as the first cypress trees appear, leave it again, to the right, on a footpath heading straight down a steep ravine. This bears left, east, down to a small valley: Vigla cistern is here. From Vigla continue south down the ravine to the Anopolis valley. This rocky ravine is well known for being 'endless' – tackle it with patience. Reverse Trek 8 for the last stage to Anopolis.

View of Trocharis from the Pachnes ridge

The Ascent of Pachnes

Trek 9. Roussies to Pachnes Summit

Grade:	C/D
Start/Finish point:	Roussies (2,050m/6,725ft) – circular walk
Access:	Trek 8 and 8a
Height:	2,453m (8,047ft)
Height gain/loss:	403m (1,322ft)
Approximate distance:	5km (3mls)
Time allowance:	2hr 20mins.

This is the easiest ascent of Pachnes, a round trip from Roussies base camp (Treks 8 and 8a). Note the daylight hours and if possible (in settled conditions) plan a late afternoon ascent, because just before sunset high mountain views look their best. Deep shadows define the hillsides and, under a dark blue sky, the light-coloured scree slopes take on a golden glow that develops into a rich orange at sunset. By twilight the magic hour has gone and slopes, robbed of shadows, revert to looking all alike. As you leave Roussies, note the valley of the north–south mule track to Katsiveli. If you lost the footpath on the descent, this valley would be your 'aiming-off' destination for the return to Roussies.

This ascent suits between July and October and months either side if the route is suitably free of snow.

If there is no one to look after your gear at Roussies, conceal it behind rocks as this is not a remote place in terms of the mountains. Taking daysack essentials including one litre of water, and allowing 3 hours minimum before sunset for the round walk, start up on the footpath to the west from Roussies pass (E4 Trail signpost).

Directions

After gaining height, traverse north-westwards to the top of the first shoulder above the mule track valley. Pachnes summit is now in view on the skyline – not the false summit that looks likely, but the group of rocks right along the ridge, 240° SW. It is not as far as it looks.

With easy gravel underfoot, gain height up this main spur by traversing across, or zigzagging up, rocky slopes, scree and gravel slopes, bands of rock, all the time heading for the ridge top by the easiest means. Cairns and waymarks guide you. At the top of the ridge, continue along it for the final pull up to the summit where there is a trig point. On a late afternoon ascent, avoid the twilight – leave the summit 1 hour 15 minutes before dark at the latest, and return down the same way.

Trek 9a. Pachnes Summit to Katsiveli

Grade:	D
Starting point:	Pachnes summit (2,453m/8,047ft)
Access:	Trek 9
Finishing point:	Katsiveli cistern (1,940m/6,374ft)
Access:	Treks 8, 8a, 4a and 5
Height loss:	513m (1,683ft)
Approximate distance:	3.5km (2mls)
Time allowance:	1hr 10mins.

This is a shepherds' route between Katsiveli and high pastures of the Pachnes massif. Katsiveli is due north of Pachnes summit, just behind the distinctive conical peak of Modaki (2,224m/7,296ft). The route passes the west side of Modaki. Clear visibility is needed as the path, which descends steeply north-east of the summit to a saddle, is not well tramped, nor very well placed for an easy 'escape' overland to the main mule track.

Trek 9b. Katsiveli to Pachnes Summit

This is Trek 9a in reverse.

Grade:	D
Starting point:	Katsiveli cistern (1,940m/6,364ft)
Access:	Treks 8, 4a and 5
Finishing point:	Pachnes summit (2,453m/8,047ft)
Access:	Trek 9
Height gain:	513m (1,683ft)
Approximate distance:	3.5km (2mls)
Time allowance:	2hrs 20mins.

Loraine Wilson on the summit of Pachnes

Directions

Leave Katsiveli on a footpath ascending the south-western rim of the valley. Turn south under the west flank of Modaki. Pachnes summit is in view, 170° SE, and the path takes the easiest route to it, following the lie of the land.

The South Coast

Trek 10. Ay. Roumeli to Souyia (E4 Trail)

Grade:	D
Starting point:	Ay. Roumeli
Access:	Coastal boat service
Finishing point:	Souyia
Access:	Coastal boat service or KTEL Souyia bus
Height loss/gain:	This is an undulating coastal footpath with two high points of 300m (984ft) and 400m (1,312ft)
Approximate distance:	18km (11mls)
Time allowance:	Ay. Roumeli to 400m (1,312ft) of first headland: 2hrs 30mins; to Klados beach: 1hr 30mins; to shepherds' huts: 2 hrs; to Tripiti Gorge: 30mins; to Turkish fort (300m/984ft)): 1hr 15mins; to Souyia: 2hrs 30mins. Total: 10hrs 15mins.

The challenging and scenically varied footpath along the rugged coastline between Ay. Roumeli and Souyia is undoubtedly one of the best wilderness walks in Crete. However, vertigo sufferers would not enjoy this route because sections of the path over steep drops are in poor condition. When bad weather affects the high mountains the south coast may be clear, and much warmer. On the other hand, even early in the year, it may be very hot. So, although you need less clothing, you have to carry enough water to suit one long stretch where there is none to be found. On the E4 Trail, this walk can be done in one very long day if you are familiar with it (it has its springtime 'regulars'), but that would be a waste. There aren't many places like this left – make the most of it by planning a 2 or 3 day trek.

As water is so scarce, avoid this route in the midsummer months, when the south coast is extremely hot, and when a storm at sea looks likely.

Route Planning. Starting from Ay. Roumeli is recommended, as in this way you head towards the good water supply at the

Eroded path on the Ay. Roumeli to Souyia trek

Tripiti Gorge ('Trip-pit-tee') and tackle the more strenuous sections first. Starting from Souyia you are faced with a steep knee-taxing descent at the end, followed by a rather exposed traverse, downhill, above Ay. Roumeli Beach, when your water supply may be very low. Another option is to start with a boat transfer from Souyia to Ay. Roumeli, which allows you a preview of the coastline. Especially avoid walking this route alone because of the inaccessible remoteness of the main section, and the poor state of the footpath.

The Route. The headland cliffs at the far end of Ay. Roumeli beach extend west to the next gorge: the Klados Gorge. To get over this headland, the footpath crosses the slope above Ay. Roumeli beach and then climbs the steep forested gully just beyond it. From Klados beach it continues west as an undulating coastal footpath to the Tripiti Gorge. After climbing steeply to a Turkish fort, on the west side of the gorge, the path descends to take up an undulating route fairly high above the shore, another 6 kilometres to Souyia.

Water (backtracking from west to east). A few minutes west of the Turkish fort, a tiny spring emerges on the footpath. The little white chapel of Profitas Ilias Tripitis along the ridge from the fort has a water cistern needed for its Panayeri festival in August, which is very popular. Participants arrive by boat. Huge crags border the Tripiti Gorge as it meets the sea in a rocky cove. A *lastico* (black pipe) from a cliff face spring supplies a shepherd's hut (perhaps not all year) and there is also a cistern beside a chapel under the east crag. At the shepherd's huts in the bay, east of the Tripiti Gorge, there are two more cisterns (private). After that, there is a small cistern beside the path in the forest above the Klados beach (very poor water at times), but this may be dry by midsummer.

Therefore, the Tripiti Gorge is the most important water point on this route. From whichever end you start, plan your supplies accordingly and, as with the high mountain treks, if your supply gets too low, do not eat because this draws on body-moisture reserves.

Directions

Pass through a gate in the fence at the top of Ay. Roumeli main street. Bear left on a steep path up through the pines to the E4 Trail pole that marks the start of the exposed-slope traverse. To some, this short section with the beach cliff yawning below may be the 'worst' on the whole route. However, on this walk to Souyia there are several stretches of one sort or another that need extra care – opinions vary on which is the worst and whether these sections are enjoyable or awful (a light backpack helps).

Beyond the traverse the path soon feels much more secure. A small rocky spur provides a last view of Ay. Roumeli. From here, lose height to negotiate a rockfall. Enter the forest of the steep gully and ascend almost right to the top of it on eroded zigzags.

Now high above the headland and other crags, the footpath leaves the trees on an undulating and contouring route around open shrub-covered hillsides (E4 Trail poles). With Ay. Roumeli out of sight, the south coast appears completely undeveloped in both directions as far as the eye can see. Inland, the inaccessible crags and gorges under Volakias, Strifomadi and Psilafi, are coming into view, forming the spectacular backdrop that accompanies much of this walk.

But first, the headland path turns north down into a pine forested, high-level valley, and then turns south again, climbing out of it to the end of the next ridge. Slippery pine needles carpet footpaths splintered by the passage of goats. At the top, mature pines and old terracing mark the start of the descent to the Klados beach. Two-thirds of the way down, pass a small rectangular concrete cistern. If it has any water, this pine-needle-contaminated liquid can be boiled up to make tea of sorts, if you wish to conserve your basic water supply.

The Klados Gorge, with its tree-capped pinnacles and its various tributary ravines, is now in full view, reminding you that every Sfakiot gorge really is different. This one ends with a wide shelf of conglomerate rock, high above a stony beach. Somehow a heavy Second World War mine shell has been brought up here from the beach. This is Ay. Roumeli goat-grazing territory (accessed by motor boat).

Leaving the cistern, descend steeply through crags to the pine-forested shelf and then bear left for the route down to the beach. At the west end of the beach, turn up the gorge bed to pick up the footpath again (E4 Trail pole). After gaining height inland above the shore, the path continues as a varied, but easy-to-follow, route for about 4 kilometres to a small bay with two shepherds' huts and cisterns. These are private cisterns and they could both be locked.

Before this bay is reached, a particularly tricky section of the route is encountered – with no easier alternatives around it. About 4 metres of path have fallen away, obliging walkers to

Beyond the exposed slopes above Ay. Roumeli

181

dash across shifting gravel to a precarious perch over a long steeply shelving slope. It is the sort of place which badly needs a steel cable handrail to make it safe.

The Tripiti Gorge is next, beyond the bay: the footpath continues around the headland on the seashore. This section would be impassable in a storm – take no risks. The possibility of this potentially disastrous situation occurring may be the reason why the cistern at the first hut, at the eastern end of the bay, is left unlocked (as of 1997). Take good care of this private water supply if you use it (see Skills section, page 24). Pass through a deep cave, an arch through the cliff, that brings you out at the chapel and cistern of the Tripiti Gorge. Huge cliffs border the river bed here where there is a shepherds' hut and a house. An astonishingly long iron ladder (condition unknown, probably corroded) is fixed like a Dolomitic *via ferrata* to the otherwise unscaleable crag above the cove. Its two lower sections have been removed so that it cannot be reached from below. Do not, therefore, think of it as an escape route in either direction if a storm blocks the seashore path.

A big free-standing rock beside the bulldozed track that goes up the gorge is level with the footpath turn-off for the steep climb to the Turkish fort. Not much further up the gorge, also on the west side of the valley, the ruins of the Dorian city of Pikilassos can be found. Goat paths from this site to the fort are strenuous – it is easier to return to the E4 Trail. *For Souyia direct:* the footpath crosses the saddle north of the fort. *For Profitis Ilias Tripitis chapel:* from the fort detour south along the forested spur. If possible, do not miss this detour as the chapel is one of the best-sited in all Crete.

On the ascent of Gingilos (Walk 3) you may have seen this tiny white chapel on the coast, far below. Here now is that view in reverse – the mountains bordering the Omalos Plateau from quite another angle. Linked directly to the south coast escarpment without a break, this south-facing flank of the western massif tumbles to the sea as a tangled mass of precipitous cliffs, inaccessible high pastures, forests and caves.

Opposite Pikilassos, faint zigzags of an ancient mule track can still be seen, climbing the spur more lately served by the iron ladder. By looking east, you can review all your efforts from the Klados Gorge. To the west, Souyia and Paleochora may, or may not, beckon depending on your inclination. Lastly, dominating the whole view, is the vast, glittering expanse of the Libyan Sea.

On the way down from the fort, shortly after passing the spring (identified by green waterweed) beside the footpath, note an old shrine that marks the correct route – it is easy to miss this short section that contours around the head of a crag. Thereafter the path to Souyia is easy to follow.

Trek 10a. Souyia to Ay. Roumeli

Note the information for Trek 10 and allow the same time schedule.

Getting to the trailhead: perched on top of a great rock buttress, Profitas Ilias Tripitis chapel can just be seen from Souyia – the limit of the view east along the coastline. The coastal footpath (E4 Trail), which once served old terracing, undulates fairly high above and a little distance inland from the seashore.

From halfway up Souyia main street, cross the river bed to pick up a bulldozed track and short cut footpaths that lead you up to the right level. A few E4 Trail poles mark the main trail, which, as far as the chapel, makes a very scenic coastal walk from Souyia. Rehydrate with a brew up at the Tripiti Gorge and resupply with a minimum of three litres of water per person from that point. Do not rely on getting water from the cistern above the Klados Gorge.

GLOSSARY

Estiatorio – offers oven cooked meals, usually in towns and waterfronts where there is a fast customer turnover

Kafeneon(ia) – coffee house serving refreshments. A village coffee house may be able to rustle up salad, omelette and chips – it depends on the skills of the proprietor and the availability of supplies

Psistaria – establishment specializing in freshly roasted meats, chips and salads

Taverna(s) – establishment that serves meals and refreshments

Nero – water

Neraki – diminutive for drinking water

Pigardi – seepage well

Potamos – river

Reeaki – stream

Sterna – rainwater collecting cistern

Vrisi – spring and also, water tap

Hora – village

Kalderimi – stone-built, paved mule track

Madares – high mountain grazing pastures

Metochi – hamlet, usually high level summer hamlet

Mitato – shepherd's mountain hut (usually called a *koumi* on the other mountain ranges of Crete)

Monopatti – footpath

Oropethio – mountain plain (Omalos, Askyfou, Niato)

Oros(i) – large mountain(s) or range

Plateia – village (or town) main square. On entering a village, ask for the *plateia* and you will find the *kafeneon* and bus stop

SOE – Special Operation Executive (a handful of Allied army intelligence agents who lived in the mountains and worked with the Cretan Resistance during the Nazi occupation 1941–45)

Thromos – road

Vouno(a) – mountain

Yeffy-rah – bridge

BOOKS – FURTHER READING

Scene of the first Bronze Age civilisation in Europe, Crete has attracted the interest of archaeologists, scientists and scholarly travellers at least since the nineteenth century. Dozens of books in Greek, English and other languages have been produced on every subject relevant to the island. A few of these, long out of print in UK, are reissued by the Efstathiades Group, Athens, as economically priced small books available locally for interested visitors. Imported books are available, but they are expensive. Foreign bookshops in the towns, and at Matala (central Crete) may stock a last copy or two of out-of-print books.

The Countryside

Stephanie Coghlan, *A Birdwatching Guide to Crete*. Arlequin Press, Chelmsford, 1996. ISBN 1900159104. Birds seen in Crete, and birdwatching areas throughout the island. Relevant to this walking guide, Chania town, Omalos, the Samaria Gorge and Lake Kourna are featured.

Oleg Polunin, *Flowers of Greece and the Balkans*. Oxford University Press, reprinted 1997. ISBN 0192819984. Useful glossary of Latin and popular names. See Chapter 2, Western Crete, for plant hunting itineraries: Omalos (Walks 1, 2), Samaria Gorge (Walk 3), Imbros gorge (Walk 21) and the Madares from Anopolis (Trek 8).

O. Rackham and J. Moody, *The Making of the Cretan Landscape*. Manchester University Press, 1996. ISBN 071903647 X/36461. Based for some time in Anopolis, a botanist and an archaeologist joined forces to produce an in-depth study covering everything to be seen in the Cretan countryside.

George Sfikas. Unassuming but useful guides: Efstathiades Group, Athens. *Birds and Mammals of Crete*, 1987 and *Wild Flowers of Crete*, 1978. Arrangement of information hardly considered, but dozens of illustrations. Also, *Trees and Shrubs of Greece*, 1979 and *The Mountains of Greece*.

N. J. Turland, L.Chilton, J. R. Press, *Flora of the Cretan Area*. The Natural History Museum, 1993. ISBN 0113100434. Crete-specific with informative introduction, but otherwise for specialists.

Cultural

Pat Cameron, *The Blue Guide: Crete*. A & C Black Ltd, 1993. ISBN 0713635886. Succinct long-lasting reference work. Car journey itineraries, but with a host of useful facts.

David MacNeil Doren, *Winds of Crete*. John Murray, 1974, reprinted Efstathiades. Living and travelling in the Cretan countryside before the rise of tourism.

Adam Hopkins, *Crete, its past, present and people*. Faber & Faber, paperback, 1977. ISBN 0571113613. Observations, history and sociology.

Two young shepherds lead the author up the garden path (to Katsiveli, Trek 8). This book may still be available locally.

H. T. Hionides, *Greek Dictionary*. Collins Gem series, UK Harper Collins, reprinted 1997. A good mini-dictionary.

Archaeology

Costis Davara, *Guide to Cretan Antiquities*. Eptalogos S.A, Athens, 1976. Helpful quick reference directory.

Alexandre Farnoux, *Knossos, the unearthing of a Legend*. Thames and Hudson, 1993. ISBN 0500300690. New Horizons series. Small size series for travel: well-presented up-to-date interpretation of the Minoan civilisation and the work of Sir Arthur Evans.

Dilys Powell, *The Villa Ariadne*. Efstathiadis, 1973. Essential memoirs concerning Sir Arthur Evan's villa, which overlooks Knossos site; its occupants over the years, including the Second World War period as headquarters for the Nazi high command.

Second World War

Anthony Beevor, *Crete, the Battle and the Resistance*. John Murray, paperback, 1991. ISBN 0719548578. Re-researched material to mark the occasion of the 50th anniversary of the Battle of Crete.

Murray Elliot, *Vassili. Lion of Crete*. Efstathiades, reprinted 1992. The story of Dudley Perkins, the New Zealander, who ran a Resistance group in the mountains above Koustoyerako (Walk 6).

George Psycoundakis, translated by Patrick Leigh Fermor, *The Cretan Runner*. UK, John Murray and Athens, Efstathiades, reprinted 1955. A young, talented, Cretan shepherd from Asi Gonia runs messages between Special Operation Executive (SOE) mountain hideouts. Said to be the only Second World War peasant memoir. Patrick Leigh Fermor's lasting tribute to the courage of Cretan Resistance volunteers who helped SOE agents.

Efstathiadis, and others, publish several other memoirs of the Battle of Crete and the Resistance years – take your pick in the local bookshops.

Novels

Nikos Kazantzakis, *Zorba the Greek*. Faber & Faber, reprinted 1987. Timeless character studies. The film was shot on the Akrotiri Peninsular.

Nikos Kazantzakis, *Freedom and Death*. Faber & Faber, reprinted 1983. 1890s Cretan fire: a spirited society including revolutionaries who sense victory is in sight, continue the struggle against Turkish rule.

Ioannis Kondylakis, *Patouchas*. Efstathiadis, 1987. Traditional shepherding life: young men forced parental decision by abducting their (hopefully willing) brides.

CICERONE GUIDES TO EUROPE

WALKING AND TREKKING IN THE ALPS

WALKING IN THE ALPS *Kev Reynolds* The popular author of many of our Alpine guide-books now draws on his vast experience to produce an outstanding comprehensive volume. Every area covered. Not for over half a century has there been anything remotely comparable. Fully illustrated. *ISBN 1 85284 261 X Large format Case bound 496pp*

CHAMONIX TO ZERMATT - The Walker's Haute Route *Kev Reynolds* The classic walk in the shadow of great peaks from Mont Blanc to the Matterhorn. In 14 stages, this is one of the most beautiful LD paths in Europe. *ISBN 1 85284 215 6 176pp*

THE GRAND TOUR OF MONTE ROSA *C.J. Wright*
Vol 1: - MARTIGNY TO VALLE DELLA SESIA (via the Italian valleys) *ISBN 1 85284 177 X 216pp*
Vol 2: - VALLE DELLA SESIA TO MARTIGNY (via the Swiss valleys) *ISBN 1 85284 178 8 182pp* The ultimate alpine LD walk which encircles most of the Pennine Alps.

TOUR OF MONT BLANC *Andrew Harper* One of the world's best walks - the circum-navigation of the Mont Blanc massif. 120 miles of pure magic, split into 11 sections. Reprinted and updated. *ISBN 1 85284 240 7 144pp PVC cover*

100 HUT WALKS IN THE ALPS *Kev Reynolds* 100 walks amid dramatic mountain scenery to high mountain huts, each with a map, photograph and route description. A fine introduction to Europe's highest mountains in France, Italy, Switzerland, Austria and Slovenia. *ISBN 1 85284 297 0 256pp*

FRANCE, BELGIUM AND LUXEMBOURG

WALKING IN THE ARDENNES *Alan Castle* 53 circular walks in this attractive area of gorges and deep cut wooded valleys, caves, castles and hundreds of walking trails. Easily accessible from the channel. *ISBN 1 85284 213 X 312pp*

THE BRITTANY COASTAL PATH *Alan Castle* The GR34, 360 miles, takes a month to walk. Easy access from UK means it can be split into several holidays. *ISBN 1 85284 185 0 296pp*

CHAMONIX - MONT BLANC - A Walking Guide *Martin Collins* In the dominating presence of Europe's highest mountain, the scenery is exceptional. A comprehensive guide to the area. *ISBN 1 85284 009 9 192pp PVC cover*

THE CORSICAN HIGH LEVEL ROUTE - Walking the GR20 *Alan Castle* The most challenging of the French LD paths - across the rocky spine of Corsica. *ISBN 1 85284 100 1 TOP New edition expected autumn 2000*

WALKING THE FRENCH ALPS: GR5 *Martin Collins* The popular trail from Lake Geneva to Nice. Split into stages, each of which could form the basis of a good holiday. *ISBN 1 85284 051 X 160pp*

WALKING THE FRENCH GORGES *Alan Castle* 320 miles through Provence and Ardèche, includes the famous gorges of the Verdon. *ISBN 1 85284 114 1 224pp*

WALKING IN THE HAUTE SAVOIE *Janette Norton* 61 walks in the pre-Alps of Chablais, to majestic peaks in the Faucigny, Haut Giffre and Lake Annecy regions. *ISBN 1 85284 196 6 312pp*

TOUR OF THE OISANS: GR54 *Andrew Harper* This popular walk around the Dauphiné massif and Écrins national park is similar in quality to the celebrated Tour of Mont Blanc. A two week itinerary covers the 270km route. *ISBN 1 85284 157 5 120pp PVC cover*

WALKING IN PROVENCE *Janette Norton* 42 walks through the great variety of Provence - remote plateaux, leafy gorges, ancient villages, monuments, quiet towns.

Provence is evocative of a gentler life. *ISBN 1 85284 293 8 248pp*

THE PYRENEAN TRAIL: GR10 *Alan Castle* From the Atlantic to the Mediterranean at a lower level than the Pyrenean High Route. 50 days but splits into holiday sections. *ISBN 1 85284 245 8 176pp*

THE TOUR OF THE QUEYRAS *Alan Castle* A 13 day walk which traverses wild but beautiful country, the sunniest part of the French Alps. Suitable for a first Alpine visit. *ISBN 1 85284 048 X 160pp*

THE ROBERT LOUIS STEVENSON TRAIL *Alan Castle* 140 mile trail in the footsteps of Stevenson's Travels with a Donkey through the Cevennes, from Le Puy to St Jean du Gard. This route is ideal for people new to walking holidays. *ISBN 1 85284 060 9 160pp*

WALKING IN THE TARENTAISE AND BEAUFORTAIN ALPS *J.W. Akitt* The delectable mountain area south of Mont Blanc includes the Vanoise National Park. 53 day walks, 5 tours between 2 and 8 day's duration, plus 40 short outings. *ISBN 1 85284 181 8 216pp*

ROCK CLIMBS IN THE VERDON - An Introduction *Rick Newcombe* An English-style guide, which makes for easier identification of the routes and descents. *ISBN 1 85284 015 3 72pp*

TOUR OF THE VANOISE *Kev Reynolds* A 10-12 day circuit of one of the finest mountain areas of France, between Mt. Blanc and the Écrins. The second most popular mountain tour after the Tour of Mont Blanc. *ISBN 1 85284 224 5 120pp*

WALKS IN VOLCANO COUNTRY *Alan Castle* Two LD walks in Central France, the High Auvergne and Tour of the Velay, in a unique landscape of extinct volcanoes. *ISBN 1 85284 092 7 208pp*

FRANCE/SPAIN

WALKS AND CLIMBS IN THE PYRENEES *Kev Reynolds* Includes the Pyrenean High Level Route. Invaluable for any backpacker or mountaineer who plans to visit this still unspoilt mountain range. (3rd Edition) *ISBN 1 85284 133 8 328pp PVC cover*

THE WAY OF ST JAMES: Le Puy to Santiago - A Cyclist's Guide *John Higginson* A guide for touring cyclists follows as closely as possible the original route but avoids the almost unrideable sections of the walkers' way. On surfaced lanes and roads. *ISBN 1 85284 274 1 112pp*

THE WAY OF ST JAMES: Le Puy to Santiago - A Walker's Guide *Alison Raju* A walker's guide to the ancient route of pilgrimage. Plus the continuation to Finisterre. *ISBN 1 85284 271 7 264pp*

THROUGH THE SPANISH PYRENEES: GR11 *Paul Lucia* An updated new edition of the long-distance trail which mirrors the French GR10 but traverses much wilder, lonlier country. With new maps and information. *ISBN 1 85284 307 1 232pp*

SPAIN AND PORTUGAL

WALKING IN THE ALGARVE *June Parker* The author of Walking in Mallorca turns her expert attention to the Algarve, with a selection of walks to help the visitor explore the true countryside. *ISBN 1 85284 173 7 168pp*

MOUNTAIN WALKS ON THE COSTA BLANCA *Bob Stansfield* An easily accessible winter walking paradise to rival Mallorca. With rugged limestone peaks and warm climate. This guide includes the 150 km Costa Blanca Mountain Way. *ISBN1 85284 165 232pp*

WALKING IN MALLORCA *June Parker.* The 3rd edition of this great classic guide, takes account of rapidly changing conditions. Revised reprint for 1999. *ISBN 1 85284 250 4 288pp PVC cover*

BIRDWATCHING IN MALLORCA *Ken Stoba* A complete guide to what to see and where to see it. *ISBN 1 85284 053 6 108pp*

THE MOUNTAINS OF CENTRAL SPAIN *Jaqueline Oglesby* Walks and scrambles in the Sierras de Gredos and Guadarrama which rise to 2600m and remain snow capped for 5 months of the year. *ISBN 1 85284 203 2 312p*

WALKING IN THE SIERRA NEVADA *Andy Walmsley* Spain's highest mountain range is a wonderland for the traveller and wilderness backpacker alike. Mountain bike routes indicated. *ISBN 1 85284 194 X 160pp*

WALKS AND CLIMBS IN THE PICOS DE EUROPA *Robin Walker* A definitive guide to these unique mountains. Walks and rock climbs of all grades. *ISBN 1 85284 033 1 232pp PVC cover*

SWITZERLAND - including parts of France and Italy

ALPINE PASS ROUTE, SWITZERLAND *Kev Reynolds* Over 15 passes along the northern edge of the Alps, past the Eiger, Jungfrau and many other renowned peaks. A 325 km route in 15 suggested stages. *ISBN 1 85284 069 2 176pp*

THE BERNESE ALPS, SWITZERLAND *Kev Reynolds* Walks around Grindelwald, Lauterbrunnen and Kandersteg dominated by the great peaks of the Oberland. *ISBN 1 85284 243 1 248pp PVC cover*

CENTRAL SWITZERLAND - A Walking Guide *Kev Reynolds* A little known but delightful area stretching from Luzern to the St Gotthard, includes Engelberg and Klausen Pass. *ISBN 1 85284 131 1 216pp PVC cover*

WALKS IN THE ENGADINE, SWITZERLAND *Kev Reynolds* The superb region to the south-east of Switzerland of the Bregaglia, Bernina Alps, and the Engadine National Park. *ISBN 1 85284 003 X 192pp PVC cover*

THE JURA: WALKING THE HIGH ROUTE *Kev Reynolds* and **WINTER SKI TRAVERSES** *R. Brian Evans.* The High Route is a long distance path along the highest crest of the Swiss Jura. In winter it is a paradise for cross-country skiers. Both sections in one volume. *ISBN 1 85284 010 2 192pp*

WALKING IN TICINO, SWITZERLAND *Kev Reynolds* Walks in the lovely Italian part of Switzerland, little known to British walkers. *ISBN 1 85284 098 6 184pp PVC cover*

THE VALAIS, SWITZERLAND - A Walking Guide *Kev Reynolds* The splendid scenery of the Pennine Alps, with such peaks as the Matterhorn, Dent Blanche, and Mont Rosa providing a perfect background. *ISBN 1 85284 151 6 224pp PVC cover*

ITALY AND SLOVENIA

ALTA VIA - HIGH LEVEL WALKS IN THE DOLOMITES *Martin Collins* A guide to some of the most popular mountain paths in Europe - Alta Via 1 and 2. *ISBN 0 902363 75 1 160pp PVC cover*

THE CENTRAL APENNINES OF ITALY - Walks, Scrambles and Climbs *Stephen Fox* The mountain spine of Italy, with secluded walks, rock climbs and scrambles on the Gran Sasso d'Italia and some of Italy's finest sport climbing crags. *ISBN 1 85284 219 9 152pp*

WALKING IN THE CENTRAL ITALIAN ALPS *Gillian Price* The Vinschgau, Ortler and Adamello regions. Little known to British walkers, certain to become popular. *ISBN 1 85284 183 4 230pp PVC cover*

WALKING IN THE DOLOMITES *Gillian Price* A comprehensive selection of walks amongst spectacular rock scenery. By far the best English guide to the area. *ISBN 1 85284 079 X PVC cover*

189

WALKING IN ITALY'S GRAN PARADISO *Gillian Price* Rugged mountains and desolate valleys with a huge variety of wildlife. Walks from short strolls to full-scale traverses. *ISBN 1 85284 231 8 200pp*

LONG DISTANCE WALKS IN THE GRAN PARADISO *J.W. Akitt* Includes Southern Valdotain. Supplements our Gran Paradiso guide by Gillian Price. Describes Alta Via 2 and the Grand Traverse of Gran Paradiso and some shorter walks. *ISBN 1 85284 247 4 168pp*

WALKS IN THE JULIAN ALPS *Simon Brown* Slovenia contains some of Europe's most attractive mountain limestone scenery. 30 walks as an introduction to the area, from valley strolls to high mountain scrambles. *ISBN 1 85284 125 7 184pp*

WALKING IN TUSCANY *Gillian Price* 50 itineraries from brief strolls to multi-day treks in Tuscany, Umbria and Latium. *ISBN 1 85284 268 7 312pp*

VIA FERRATA SCRAMBLES IN THE DOLOMITES *Höfler/Werner Translated by Cecil Davies* The most exciting walks in the world. Wires, stemples and ladders enable the 'walker' to enter the climber's vertical environment. *ISBN 1 85284 089 7 248pp PVC cover*

OTHER MEDITERRANEAN COUNTRIES

THE ATLAS MOUNTAINS *Karl Smith* Trekking in the mountains of north Africa. Practical and comprehensive. *ISBN 1 85284 258 X 136pp PVC cover*

WALKING IN CYPRUS *Donald Brown* Without a guide getting lost in Cyprus is easy. Donald Brown shares undiscovered Cyprus with 26 easy to moderate routes for walkers. *ISBN 1 85284 195 8 144pp*

THE MOUNTAINS OF GREECE - A Walker's Guide *Tim Salmon* Hikes of all grades from a month-long traverse of the Pindos to day hikes on the outskirts of Athens. *ISBN 1 85284 108 7 PVC cover*

THE MOUNTAINS OF TURKEY *Karl Smith* Over 100 treks and scrambles with detailed route descriptions of all the popular peaks. Includes Ararat. *ISBN 1 85284 161 3 184pp PVC cover*

TREKS AND CLIMBS IN WADI RUM, JORDAN *Tony Howard* The world's foremost desert climbing and trekking area. Increasingly popular every year as word of its quality spreads. *ISBN 1 85284 254 7 252pp A5 Card cover*

JORDAN - Walks, Treks, Caves, Climbs, Canyons in Pella, Ajlun, Moab, Dana, Petra and Rum *Di Taylor & Tony Howard* The first guidebook to the superlative routes found in Jordan's recently formed Nature Reserves. These are walks, treks, caves and climbs described in this little known landscape by the authors of our Wadi Rum guide. *ISBN 1 85284 278 4 192pp A5*

THE ALA DAG, Climbs and Treks in Turkey's Crimson Mountains *O.B. Tüzel* The best mountaineering area in Turkey. *ISBN 1 85284 112 5 296pp PVC cover*

Get ready for take off

Adventure Travel helps you to go 'outdoors over there'

More ideas, information, advice and entertaining features on overseas trekking, walking and backpacking than any other outdoor magazine – guaranteed. Available from good newsagents or by subscription – 6 issues £15

Adventure Travel Magazine   T: 01789 488166

Climber

IF YOU LIKE ADVENTUROUS ACTIVITIES ON MOUNTAINS OR HILLS YOU WILL ENJOY

Climber

MOUNTAINEERING / HILLWALKING / TREKKING / ROCK CLIMBING / SCRAMBLING IN BRITAIN AND ABROAD

AVAILABLE FROM NEWSAGENTS, OUTDOOR EQUIPMENT SHOPS, OR BY SUBSCRIPTION (6-12 MONTHS) from

WARNER GROUP PUBLICATIONS PLC
THE MALTINGS, WEST STREET, BOURNE, LINCS PE10 9PH
Tel: 01778 393313 Fax: 01778 394748
ISDN: 01778 423059 email: Sam.a@warners.co.uk

mountain / sports incorporating 'Mountain INFO'

Britain's liveliest and most authoritive magazine for mountaineers, climbers and ambitious hillwalkers. Gives news and commentary from the UK and worldwide, backed up by exciting features and superb colour photography.   *OFFICIAL MAGAZINE*

Have you read it yet?

Available monthly from your newsagent or specialist gear shop.

Call 01533 460722 for details

BRITISH
MOUNTAINEERING
COUNCIL

THE WALKERS' MAGAZINE

THE GREAT OUTDOORS

COMPULSIVE MONTHLY READING FOR
ANYONE INTERESTED IN WALKING

*AVAILABLE FROM NEWSAGENTS,
OUTDOOR EQUIPMENT SHOPS, OR BY SUBSCRIPTION
(6-12 MONTHS) from*

**CALEDONIAN MAGAZINES LTD,
6th FLOOR, 195 ALBION STREET, GLASGOW G1 1QQ
Tel: 0141 302 7700 Fax: 0141 302 7799
ISDN No: 0141 302 7792 e-mail: info@calmags.co.uk**